TEXTS AND CONTEXTS

Series Editors:
Gail Ashton and Fiona McCulloch

Texts and Contexts is a series of clear, concise and accessible introductions to key literary fields and concepts. The series provides the literary, critical, historical context for texts and authors in a specific literary area in a way that introduces a range of work in the field and enables further independent study and reading.

Other titles available in the series:

Children's Literature in Context, Fiona McCulloch
The Contemporary American Novel in Context, Andrew Dix, Brian Jarvis and Paul Jenner
Medieval English Romance in Context, Gail Ashton
Postcolonial Literatures in Context, Julie Mullaney

TEXTS AND CONTEXTS

The Victorian Novel in Context

GRACE MOORE

Continuum International Publishing Group

The Tower Building
11 York Road
London
SE1 7NX

80 Maiden Lane
Suite 704
New York
NY 10038

www.continuumbooks.com

British Library Cataloguing-in-Publication Data
A catalogue record for this book is available from the British Library.

ISBN: HB: 978-1-8470-6488-2
PB: 978-1-8470-6489-9

Library of Congress Cataloging-in-Publication Data
Moore, Grace, 1974-
The Victorian novel in context / Grace Moore.
p. cm. – (Texts and contexts)
Includes bibliographical references and index.
ISBN 978-1-84706-488-2 (hardcover) – ISBN 978-1-84706-489-9 (pbk.) – ISBN 978-1-4411-2413-5 (ebook (pdf)) – ISBN 978-1-4411-1267-5 (ebook (epub))
1. English fiction–19th century–History and criticism.
2. Literature and society–England–History–19th century. I. Title.

PR871.M66 2012
823'.809–dc23

2011046643

Typeset by Newgen Imaging Systems Pvt Ltd, Chennai, India
Printed and bound in India

CONTENTS

Series Editor's Preface vi
Acknowledgements vii

Introduction 1

PART ONE Contexts 7
1 Victorianism 9
2 Literary context 37

PART TWO Texts 49
3 Readings of key texts 51

PART THREE Wider contexts 111
4 Critical context 113
5 Afterlives and adaptations 135

Bibliography 156
Index 169

SERIES EDITOR'S PREFACE

Texts and Contexts offers clear and accessible introductions to key literary fields. Each book in the series outlines major historical, social, cultural and literary contexts that impact upon its specified area. It engages contemporary responses to selected texts and authors through a variety of exemplary close readings, by exploring the ideas of seminal theorists and/or a range of critical approaches, as well as examining adaptations and afterlives. Readers are encouraged to make connections and ground further independent study through 'Review', 'Reading' and 'Research' sections at the end of most chapters, which offer selected bibliographies, web resources, open and closed questions, discussion topics and pointers for extended research.

ACKNOWLEDGEMENTS

I am first and foremost grateful to the series editors Gail Ashton and Fiona McCulloch, as well as Colleen Coalter and Rachel Eisenhauer at Continuum, who have been supremely patient in waiting for me to finish this book. There have been a number of times when this project seemed to have been jinxed, and I am especially grateful to Gail for her compassionate understanding of the clash of responsibilities that comes with combining motherhood, academe and a travelling partner. I owe a huge debt to Kristine Moruzi (now of the University of Alberta), who worked as my research assistant to format and finalize another project when a severely broken hand left me completely incapacitated and unable to work on this book or anything else. Her cheerful diligence during the five months I spent in plaster, and the many more months of physio that followed, allowed me to turn back to the Victorian novel sooner than would otherwise have been possible.

At the University of Melbourne, I owe deep thanks to Barb Creed for allowing me a semester of teaching relief and for her personal and professional generosity during her time as Head of School. As always, I'm grateful for the support of colleagues in the English and Theatre program at Melbourne, particularly Deirdre Coleman, Ken Gelder, Anne Maxwell, Stephanie Trigg, Clara Tuite and Denise Varney. Peter Otto has been amazingly supportive and no words can convey my gratitude for the help and guidance he has given, particularly over the last five years. Some of the work for this book was completed with the assistance of an Arts Faculty Teaching Support Fellowship, for which I am grateful.

Steve Wasserman told me 20 years ago that I should read more Dickens, and I'm glad to have the chance to thank him for this and other life-altering recommendations. Chris Brooks passed onto me his great passion for the industrial novel and, as always, I have missed his vast knowledge, good humour and infectious enthusiasm. I wish he had been here to discuss this book as I was writing it.

Sofia Ahlberg, Cassandra Atherton, Claire Knowles, Owen and Indigo Jones, Deborah Denenholz Morse, Cathy Scott, Charlotte Smith, Lucy Sussex, Clara Tuite (again) and Tamara Wagner have all offered friendship, distraction and, in several cases, insights into the Victorian novel. I am especially grateful to my friend Rowena Fowler and greatly miss our regular conversations about the Victorians. Like so many other Victorian scholars across the globe, I continue to be indebted to the VICTORIA-L list, its members and its moderator, Patrick Leary, as well as Patrick McCarthy's valuable DICKENS-L discussion list. I would also like to thank Miriam Elizabeth Burstein for permission to quote from her blog, 'The Little Professor'.

Andrew and Felix Robinson have, between them, done everything possible to prevent this book from being written. Felix, in particular, has moved from chicken pox to full-blown hospitalization in a bid to remind me of where my priorities lie. I'm grateful to Andrew for jetting in from Brisbane, en route to Malaysia, to give me a few last days of peace in which to work on the final manuscript and for the hard questions he has asked about the nineteenth century. This book is for both of them, with my love.

INTRODUCTION

When you think about the Victorians, how do you envision them? There are icons of the Victorian age that, for many, immediately spring to mind: Queen Victoria, the vast imperial map, coloured red to reflect British territories, inventions like the electric telegraph, and the enormous three-volume novels that went on for hundreds of pages. Not everybody holds such a positive view of the Victorians and many other readers might characterize the period as dreary, dark and repressed. The Modernist writer Virginia Woolf adopted such a position in her novel *Orlando* (1928), in which the movement from the eighteenth to the nineteenth century was characterized by gloom. The weather underwent an instant change and damp began to creep into everyone and everything. Woolf's depiction of the oppressive nineteenth century goes on for several pages, as she deflates the Victorians through layers of wicked, playful satire. No aspect of Victorian culture is safe from her attack, as her narrator passes withering commentary on everything from horticulture to gender relations. Her tone is mocking, as she uses hyperbole to poke fun at an entire historical period, noting at one stage, 'The life of the average woman was a succession of childbirths. She married at nineteen and had fifteen or eighteen children by the time she was thirty' (229).

Woolf provides a useful entry point to considering the Victorian novel, because although she approached it with sardonic contempt, it was a source of inspiration, anxiety and oppression to her at different stages of her career. As I shall discuss in Chapter Five, Woolf had her own creative agenda when she attempted to lampoon the Victorians in her fiction, but the fact that she needed to do so at all should alert us to the monumental influence and importance of the Victorian legacy and, in particular, the Victorian novel.

The novel is a vital resource for anyone wanting to understand more about Victorian culture and society. Victorians with leisure time (namely those from the middle and upper classes) read voraciously and the novel became an important medium for speaking to and influencing those with power. It is as difficult to generalize about the Victorian novel as it is to neatly sum up the Victorian period. George Levine argues that the term 'Victorian novel' 'is an all-inclusive and therefore crude category', before going on to remind us that this catch-all term covers a whole sequence of different forms, including 'romance, sensation novel, industrial novel, *Bildungsroman*, fantasy, historical novel, multiplot novel, autobiographical novel, adventure novel, realist novel' (2008: 1). The books the Victorians wrote were as diverse as their fascinating society, and this guide will lead you through some of the dialogues between fiction and reality and some of the changes in the shape and format of the novel.

Before embarking on a discussion of the Victorian novel, we should note that the Victorians read very differently from the way we read today and that this inevitably changed how they engaged with texts. Whereas we are accustomed to being able to sit down with a novel, staying up all night to finish it if it is a particularly riveting read, the Victorians often read novels in parts and would have to wait for the next instalment to be published. As a consequence, cliffhangers created much more suspense and excitement than they possibly can for readers who need only turn the page to discover the hero's fate. Those who wrote in instalments had to pace their stories to engage readers and to keep them coming back for more. They made liberal use of dramatic chapter endings, often leaving characters in dangerous or thrilling situations so that the reader would *have* to buy the next edition of the journal or magazine in which the story appeared. Of course, while the novelist who wrote in parts was always writing under the threat of dwindling circulation, he or she could also turn the form to advantage, adapting the narrative according to public interest and changing the plot direction if need be.

Reading in the nineteenth century was a much more communal activity than it is today, with tens of thousands of readers across the country (and sometimes across the globe) all reading the same story at the same time. Novels were widely discussed at social events, and readers would enjoy speculating about what would happen next in the latest serial. For many, particularly the middle classes, reading was an all-consuming activity and of central importance to those with leisure time.

Focusing on six representative texts from the early, mid- and late-Victorian periods, this guide will introduce you to some of the debates and contextual issues underpinning the Victorian novel, highlighting the rise of realist writing and the interplay between fiction and real life. The novels I have selected reflect changes and developments in writing and representation, but they cannot possibly convey the rich variety and diversity that characterizes Victorian writing. You should therefore consider this book as an introduction, which will assist you in identifying some of the key debates and concerns surrounding the Victorian novel, but which is in no way a definitive or exhaustive account. As you move on to read more Victorian fiction, you will discover just how difficult it is to make totalizing comments about a form that was endlessly developing and evolving.

As one of the first Victorian novels (it was published serially between 1837 and 1839), Charles Dickens' *Oliver Twist* is a transitional text, offering a helpful bridge between the comic novel of the eighteenth century and the social reform novel of the nineteenth. Charlotte Brontë's *Jane Eyre* (1847) takes itself much more seriously as a piece of realist fiction and, while Dickens combines humour with a call for urgent social reform, Brontë's writing is characterized by her protagonist's intense inner life and the attention she pays to gender issues. Elizabeth Gaskell's *North and South* (1855) represents the form known as the 'industrial novel', a work engaged with the challenges encountered by those living in manufacturing cities. As a Unitarian minister's wife, living in Manchester, Gaskell had first-hand experience of some of the privations suffered by those employed in factories and used her fiction to draw attention to the appalling conditions endured by the workforce. As its title suggests, *North and South* explores the enormous differences between life in the great new Northern cities and the quieter pastoral South. George Eliot in *The Mill on the Floss* (1860) is similarly engaged in representing the tensions between urban expansion and a more agrarian existence, although her novel is also deeply concerned with gender politics and the wasted potential of her heroine, Maggie Tulliver. These mid-Victorian authors make an interesting point of comparison, not least because they were aware of one another's work and sometimes even involved in it. Elizabeth Gaskell and Charlotte Brontë were friends and, following Brontë's death in 1855, Gaskell became her first biographer.

Gaskell wrote for Dickens' journal *Household Words* and Dickens oscillated between admiration for his 'Scheherezade' and frustration that she could not constrain her writing to the demands of the periodical format, writing to his assistant W. H. Wills, 'if we put in more, every week, of *North and South* than we did of *Hard Times*, we shall ruin *Household Words*. Therefore it must at all hazards be kept down' (Dickens, *Letters* 7: 403). Dickens also corresponded with both George Eliot and her partner G. H. Lewes, although he was never able to persuade Eliot to write for him, in spite of his best efforts.

Writing much later in the century, Thomas Hardy is likely to have been familiar with the work of his mid-Victorian predecessors, although he is often aligned with more modern writers. We know that Hardy was particularly influenced by George Eliot's writing, to the degree that when *Far From the Madding Crowd* was serialized in the *Cornhill* magazine in 1874, many readers believed that it was Eliot's work. Like Eliot, Hardy was engaged in exploring a rural community's response to change and the novel I have chosen to discuss here, *The Mayor of Casterbridge* (1886), exemplifies some of the tensions between the old world and the new. Bram Stoker's *Dracula* (1897) is, however, radically different from any of the other texts and I have included it in this book to demonstrate how the novel changed its form, content and direction in the closing years of the nineteenth century. While its supernatural focus on vampires and the un-dead places it in opposition to the other solidly realist novels we will examine, there is nevertheless a remarkable overlap between some of the topical issues, including gender and the city, that Stoker chooses to address. I will not discuss each novel in every single section; rather, I shall focus on the texts that are most relevant to the topic under discussion and you may wish to dip into individual parts according to your interest.

This book's structure follows the format for the series. Part One introduces the selected novels and highlights some key social, political and historical events to demonstrate the strong connection between politics and writing for many Victorian novelists. Part Two is structured thematically and focuses on close readings of the works, in places offering comparisons between different authors and at other points focusing intensively on a single text. Part Three surveys six differing, yet influential, critical responses to the primary texts, including work by Gillian Beer, Gayatri Chakravorty Spivak, Terry Eagleton, Michel Foucault, Ralph Pite and Mary Poovey. Chapter Five, which is the final chapter, examines the role of Victorian culture in contemporary society, paying attention to the backlash against Victorianism in the early twentieth century, before going on to discuss reworkings of Victorian texts and Neo-Victorianism more generally.

PART ONE
Contexts

CHAPTER ONE
Victorianism

The phrase 'the Victorian period', although a useful shorthand, does not really reflect the dynamic changes that took place in Britain between Victoria's succession to the throne in 1837 and her death in 1901. 'Victorianism' is becoming an increasingly contested term as scholars argue that it obscures the many changes that British culture and society underwent during the nineteenth century. Kate Flint, writing of her uneasiness with the term 'Victorian', argues that to think in terms of 'periodization' is to restrict our understanding of the continuity between historical periods and our own connection to the nineteenth century. Flint urges us to be alert to the cultural baggage embedded in the word 'Victorian' and to be aware of its limitations (2005: 239). Joseph Bristow adopts a similar position asserting that – historically sandwiched between Romanticism and Modernism – Victorianism resists theorization (2004: 2) as it is an historical period rather than a philosophical or ideological movement. He also notes, importantly, that the term 'Victorian' did not enter broad circulation until the 1870s (3), so that in using the term to discuss the duration of Queen Victoria's reign, we are, in fact, misappropriating it.

While I share Bristow's and Flint's discomfort with the general nature of the term 'Victorian', it has entered our common vocabulary to signify the literary works produced while Victoria was on the throne. I agree that 'Victorianism' needs to be scrutinized and interrogated, yet it remains a highly useful form of shorthand with which to discuss the era. As a result, although I will use the term throughout this book, I ask you to reflect upon its meaning and usefulness as you read and consider the novels, particularly when you come to the sections on Neo-Victorianism and Afterlives in Part Three.

Social and cultural context

A reforming age

The Victorian period was an era of both reform and agitation. Although it sometimes moved slowly, legislation attempted to respond to some of the challenges of industrialism and the ways in which a shift in the balance of power and wealth had reconfigured class relations. One of the first attempts to reflect the rise to power of increasingly wealthy manufacturers was the Great Reform Bill of 1832. Many historians believe that this Act of Parliament separated middle-class radicals from working-class agitators so that there was no longer an incentive for discontented members of the bourgeoisie to whip up discontent within the working classes, whose sheer numbers posed a threat when they were encouraged to take to the streets.

By today's standards, the 1832 Reform Act does not seem at all radical, in that it only enfranchised a very limited and privileged sector of the population. Male owners of property with a value of more than ten pounds per annum were given the right to vote, although this translated into roughly only one in six men. A woman had no electoral rights and it was not until 1928 that women's entitlement to vote was brought into line with that of men. The 1832 Act was also important because it redrew the boundaries of electoral constituencies so that they were divided more equally. So-called rotten boroughs were abolished, so that it was no longer possible for a town or village with few residents, like Old Sarum near Salisbury, to have its own Member of Parliament. Seats were redistributed so that the new metropolitan centres devoted to manufacturing, like Bradford, Leeds, Halifax or Manchester, were better represented in the House of Commons.

While 1832 is obviously not strictly a part of the Victorian period, the Reform Act is generally considered to reflect the spirit of the age and the Victorians' impetus for improvement. The year 1832 was only the beginning in terms of widening the electorate, and the Reform Act of 1867, along with the Representation of the People Act (1884), gradually began to include working people. The 1867 Act extended the vote to include all male householders, while the 1884 Bill extended it still further. The philosopher and critic

Thomas Carlyle fearfully described the Act of 1867 as 'shooting Niagara' (Carlyle, 1867), believing that it would open the floodgates of political anarchy and overturn the structure of society. In fact, a large number of men (estimated at as many as 40 per cent) remained disenfranchised, since both Bills continued to connect the right to vote to material wealth.

The city

The poet William Wordsworth famously complained of London in Book Seven of *The Prelude* (1805 and 1850) that 'The face of every one/That passes by me is a mystery' and this observation encapsulates the traumas associated with urban living in the Victorian age. As the most advanced industrial nation, Britain was in uncharted territory when it came to coping with the extraordinary demographic changes brought about by the rise of capitalism, and one of the real upheavals associated with industrialism was the massive movement of people from the country to the city. Raymond Williams very helpfully reminds us of just how new this way of life was with his assertion that '[b]y the end of the 1840s the English were the first predominantly urban people in the long history of human societies' (1970: 9). Williams emphasizes the 'sense of crisis' that prevailed as society sought to come to terms with the strangeness of the industrial world and a reconfigured way of life.

Increasingly, for the Victorians, the city was 'just over the horizon', and a comparison of the world of *Oliver Twist* to that of Bram Stoker's *Dracula* offers some idea of the rapid changes to urban life in the nineteenth century. With more than four million inhabitants, London was a considerably larger place in 1897 than it was at the beginning of the nineteenth century, when its population was 865,000. By the 1890s, electric trains ferried passengers across the capital on the underground, offering in the process a type of subterranean metaphor for the infernal characteristics of the more notorious areas of the capital city. Outlying suburbs were being subsumed into the metropolis, and London was transformed into a global capital. However, during Victoria's reign London's dominance was challenged by the rise of northern manufacturing cities to the extent that, as Richard D. Altick has commented, by 1891 there were 23 cities with populations above

100,000, compared with just one (London) at the beginning of the century (76).

Metropolitan life was certainly beginning to impinge upon communities like Thomas Hardy's Casterbridge and George Eliot's St. Ogg's, where the type of impersonal capitalism represented by the ruthless Lawyer Wakem was displacing business transactions conducted on trust between friends. Indeed, even in an early novel like *Oliver Twist* the characters are notably mobile, with Fagin appearing suddenly to terrorize Oliver in his country idyll at the end of chapter 34 and Bill Sikes walking to and from London in his bid to escape apprehension for Nancy's murder.

The fact that the majority of British subjects now lived in urban conglomerations (by 1914 more than 70 per cent of the population had migrated to towns or cities) meant that the realist novel was largely focused on metropolitan life. Novels representing the countryside often did so from a position of nostalgia for a way of life that was lost or, as in the case of Eliot and Hardy, they demonstrated the expansionism of city life and values. The industrial novel in particular was concerned with the struggles of urban inhabitants, at the same time introducing the reader to the unfamiliar world of the factory town with its discomforting convergence of dazzling success stories and extraordinary misery.

Poverty

Thomas Carlyle famously described poverty as 'the Hell of which most modern Englishmen are most afraid' (in Bourke, 2005: 27) and in a world without the types of welfare systems we know today, poverty was a truly terrifying prospect. The fear of poverty and its consequences haunts the Victorian novel and is a spectre on the horizon for many characters, just as it was for people in the real world. Realist writers sought to highlight the vast gulf between the wealthy and the destitute and a new form of novel emerged, which we know today as the 'social problem novel' because it drew attention to areas in need of reform. Charles Dickens was one of the pioneers of the social reform novel, which sought to make readers aware of the enormous chasm between the lives of the wealthy and of those in poverty. Benjamin Disraeli famously wrote of the 'two nations' in Britain, the rich and the poor, in his 1841 novel *Sybil*, and his representation of the poor as completely and utterly 'other' is a helpful way of thinking about the divisions between classes and the mutual distrust that resulted from industrialism (1845: 66).

One of the most striking aspects of the nineteenth-century realist novel is its graphic depiction of urban poverty. While the growth of an industrial economy created unprecedented national prosperity and enabled middle-class factory owners to rise to social and economic dominance, Britain's success did not extend to every sector of society. Indeed, in 1842 nearly one and a half million of the sixteen million inhabitants of England and Wales were classed as 'paupers' (Smith, 1980: 5). While the middle class became increasingly prosperous, the working classes lived in fear of the effects of the 1834 Poor Law Amendment Act, which effectively criminalized poverty and hindered those who had slipped into poverty from re-establishing themselves.

The Act abolished 'outdoor relief' whereby those who had fallen on hard times would apply to their local parish for assistance and would be helped to stay in their own homes and to get themselves back on their feet. Embodying the principles of the Utilitarian philosopher Jeremy Bentham, the Poor Law Amendment Act aimed to centralize aid and to make sure that people would only seek help as a last resort. Workhouses were established as a means of grouping the poor together and administering charity efficiently and cheaply. These institutions became notorious for the appalling conditions in which the poor were housed; families were separated from one another and inmates were subjected to a regime of hard work and a subsistence diet. The workhouses quickly became a source of great terror to working people, and so great was their resemblance to jails, that they were nicknamed 'Bastilles' after the notorious French prison. The historian Gertrude Himmelfarb has explained that the changes brought about by the Poor Law Amendment Act created a distinction between those who were simply poor and those who were classified as 'paupers' (1984: 147). To become a 'pauper' and to surrender to the workhouse involved great social stigma, whereas to be simply 'poor' was regarded as acceptable, and the 'poor' were often celebrated for their hard work and virtuous thrift. Charles Dickens encapsulated the working-class fear of the workhouse in his last completed novel *Our Mutual Friend* (1865), in which the character Betty Higden endures terrible poverty and hardship but stubbornly refuses to enter a workhouse.

She eventually dies far from home, having decided that it would be better to run away than to risk spending her final days imprisoned in the dreaded 'House'. Indeed, as the chronicler of the 'real Oliver Twist', John Waller has noted, 'Pride kept many out' (2005: 33), thus reminding readers that Betty was not alone in her refusal to accept the state's severe brand of charity.

The film director David Lean attempted to translate the horror of the workhouse into modern terms with the opening scenes of his 1948 adaptation of *Oliver Twist*. Drawing upon recent events in Europe, Lean's eerie first shots of the workhouse in a storm – viewed through brambles that look like barbed wire – stress its resemblance to a concentration camp, drawing subtle parallels between the starved orphans who were thrown on the mercy of the parish and the victims of the atrocities of the Holocaust. Lean's decision emphasizes just how hungry and poorly treated many of the children in Oliver's position would have been, and it's important for us, as well-fed readers, to understand the degree of abuse that Dickens was exposing.

Chartism

The 1832 Reform Act succeeded in easing tensions between the manufacturing classes and those who had traditionally wielded political power, namely the landed gentry. However, it did nothing to appease the working classes, and the early years of Queen Victoria's reign were troubled by hunger, disease and political unrest. One of the most influential movements to emerge from this turbulent climate was the Chartist Movement, described by Asa Briggs as 'the greatest movement of popular protest in British history' (1998: 1). The Chartists reacted angrily to the 1832 Reform Act's neglect of the working man and put together a 'people's charter', demanding parliamentary reform, which was published and presented to Parliament in May 1838. The Chartists themselves were skilled artisans and working-class radicals, and the six points they demanded were:

- A vote for each man over the age of 20 (note that votes for women did not form part of the agenda)
- Secret ballots

- Abolition of the property qualification to vote
- Payment of Members of Parliament
- Equal size of parliamentary constituencies
- Annual parliaments

The Charter was rejected by Parliament (only 46 MPs voted in its favour, the other 235 were opposed to it), even though it had been signed by well over a million people. The Chartist leaders had threatened to call a general strike if the document was turned down, so they were rounded up and arrested during the marches that followed the presentation. Violence ensued, including the so-called Newport Rising in which Chartist demonstrators marched on Newport Prison to demand the release of their leaders – troops were called in and 24 people were killed, while another 40 were injured. Nevertheless, the Charter was presented again in 1842 and for a final time in 1848.

The Chartists' activities were facilitated by a campaign for a 'Cheap and Honest Press' in the early 1830s, demanding the reduction in taxes on the so-called pauper press. Briggs suggests that when the Whig government reduced stamp duty on newspapers to a penny in March 1836, it triumphed in its ongoing efforts to drive a wedge between working- and middle-class radicals by reducing the prices of middle-class publications, while at the same time raising the cost of the working man's newspaper (27–8). The energies surrounding this campaign were then subsumed into the Chartist Movement, knitting concerns about freedom of expression together with working-class social and political demands.

While the idea of a Chartist Movement points to unity and solidarity, the Chartists were a very diverse group of people, representing different regional concerns and priorities, but as Briggs has noted, they were brought together by 'the stimulus of economic distress' (52). Some Chartists were committed to establishing freedom of the press, while in the 1840s others were deeply concerned with repealing the bread tax, which stemmed from the despised Corn Laws. These laws were a protective measure designed to reduce the importation of grain from overseas. It was prohibited to import grain until the price per quarter reached four pounds. While the law was of benefit to growers, it penalized the poorest people, for whom bread was a staple food. The plot of *The*

Mayor of Casterbridge takes place prior to the abolition of the Corn Laws, showing through the characters Michael Henchard and Donald Farfrae how a fortune could be made or lost through speculating on harvests and the price of grain.

The Chartists believed that under a democracy it would be impossible for unjust legislation to be carried and while many feared the more violent, militant wings of the group, others were afraid of what would happen if the Chartists gained political power. Thomas Carlyle captured some of the sheer terror the Chartists inspired when he commented,

> Chartism means the bitter discontent grown fierce and mad, the wrong condition therefore of the wrong disposition of the Working Classes of England. It is a new name for a thing which has had many names, which will yet have many. The matter of Chartism is weighty, deep-rooted, far-extending: did not begin yesterday; will by no means end this day or tomorrow. (1980: 151–2)

Carlyle here recognizes that Chartism is certainly not a new phenomenon and that it will not disappear suddenly. The movement went into decline after 1848, when the Charter was presented to Parliament for the last time, although this was partly because of a government commission that discredited a number of the group's leaders. The energies behind Chartism were gradually channelled into other causes, including trade unionism.

The Chartists appealed to a number of writers, particularly those involved in depicting the conditions of the working classes. Although there are no Chartists in *Oliver Twist*, Charles Dickens represented them with a mixture of fear and sensitivity in *The Old Curiosity Shop* (1840–41), while Elizabeth Gaskell had first-hand experience of them, as a Manchester resident. Gaskell's novel *Mary Barton* appeared in 1848, and amidst its graphic representations of starving factory workers, it included representations of trade unionists as well as depicting the character John Barton's hopelessness when the Chartist delegation, of which he is a member, fails to obtain the sympathies of Westminster politicians. Gaskell also transcribed Chartist poems and songs into *Mary Barton* in a bid to help her middle-class readers hear the authentic voices and sufferings of the people. Importantly, while *Mary Barton* focuses almost entirely on the miseries of the underclass, in *North and South* Gaskell takes pains to highlight the difficulties of the factory owners, showing a society in which everyone is struggling and in which all would benefit from improved communications and understanding.

Gaskell's attitude to the people is at times ambivalent and reflects her position as a member of the middle class. By today's standards, both Gaskell and Charles Dickens would fall short in their radicalism as although they were both deeply sympathetic to those living in poverty, they were both challenged and slightly fearful when working men and women became politically agitated. While no political revolution occurred in Britain in the nineteenth century (despite unrest across Europe particularly in 1848, the so-called year of revolutions), many members of the middle classes feared a similar uprising. These anxieties are often expressed in novels through frenetic crowd scenes in which individual identities became subsumed. Although it is a loaded term, when discontented members of the working class occupied the streets in this way, they were often perceived as a 'mob', and regardless of whether their intentions were peaceful, many middle-class bystanders were afraid. John Plotz has helpfully pointed out some of the difficulties in examining and understanding the crowd, particularly when it is represented by middle-class writers. Plotz writes of an 'ongoing battle to define what a crowd did' (2000: 7), and in approaching crowd scenes we, as readers, need to maintain an awareness of each author's positioning in relation to the people who have taken to the streets. Crowds give Victorian novels their energy, but they are also a source of fear and uncertainty for middle-class radicals committed to reform in moderation.

Money

One of the dominant plots of the Victorian novel is the getting and losing of money. Barbara Weiss in *The Hell of the English: Bankruptcy and the Victorian Novel* has highlighted the connections between the fear of poverty and 'the destruction of the family circle' (1986: 58), arguing for the underlying fragility of the Victorian middle-class home. Gaskell's *North and South* highlights the suddenness with which fortunes could be won or lost, with Thornton's business failure being rapidly succeeded by Margaret's legacy, thus fortuitously allowing him to continue his trade. The realist novel reflects the rapidity with which people rose to prominence or fell into obscurity in Victorian Britain, highlighting the unreliability of money made in trade or in financial speculation, and emphasizing the fundamental instability of middle-class power.

Charles Dickens in *Little Dorrit* (1855–57) and Anthony Trollope in *The Way We Live Now* (1875) both depicted the far-reaching consequences of financial fraud through their respective villains Mr. Merdle and Augustus Melmotte. Mirroring the behaviour of men like the real-life fraudster, John Sadleir, Merdle and Melmotte persuade large numbers of people from all walks of life to invest their savings in illusory money making schemes, both committing suicide when their deceptions can no longer be sustained. Sensational though their scams may be, the behaviour of these two fictional villains mirrored a sequence of high-profile swindles, which rocked the stability of Victorian Britain. George Hudson, the so-called railway king, for instance, began his career through investing in the building of railway tracks, connecting cities across the North of England. By 1844, he was responsible for the laying of over one thousand miles of track and became a Member of Parliament. However, Hudson was ruined overnight – as were those who had sunk their life savings into his business – partly because he had overvalued his shares and manipulated their prices, and partly because he had been bribing government officials with his investors' money.

Hudson's story is far from an isolated incident and many middle-class Victorians and members of the gentry were taken in by fraudulent share schemes. One of the reasons for the large numbers of governesses in the 1840s and 1850s stemmed from large-scale bank failures in the 1830s, leaving educated middle-class women without resources and in search of a respectable profession. Some became dressmakers or milliners, while many others became governesses, usually drawing a low salary and occupying an ambiguous position within the household, since they were not family members, yet nor were they servants. The gaining and keeping of money was an extremely touchy subject in the Victorian novel, as it was in society, and one that it was not always considered genteel to discuss. The dubious origins of rapidly made money were often concealed and, interestingly, at a time of intense fiscal speculation, novels featuring gamblers and gambling became highly popular, acknowledging on one level the awkward connections between financial risk and gaming.

Education

A number of Victorian novels are concerned with representing and critiquing education. The nineteenth century saw a sequence of educational reforms, which were often tied to legislation surrounding factories and children's working hours. Although it predates the Victorian period, the Factory Act of 1833 attempted to secure a minimum of two hours of schooling each day for children working in factories, while also limiting the number of hours they spent at work. Further reforms included Forster's Elementary Education Act of 1870, which implemented primary schooling for all children under the age of 12 – attendance became compulsory after 1880.

By the end of the century, more teachers were being trained (Mina Harker in *Dracula* is an assistant school mistress) and more schools were being built, with education gradually coming to form an integral part of childhood for the working classes. While philanthropists were concerned with the instruction of working children, a number of social reformers including Mary Buss and Dorothea Beale campaigned for the education of girls. The debate intensified in the closing decades of the nineteenth century, with the emergence of the New Woman and her demands for equality of education. There was, however, a great deal of conflict throughout Victoria's reign as to exactly what constituted a suitable education for a woman. John Ruskin debated this question in his 1864 lecture 'Of Queen's Gardens' (published in print form in 1865) in which he considered the roles of men and women in relation to each other. In speaking of an education suitable for a woman, he commented:

> The first of our duties to her – no thoughtful persons now doubt this – is to secure for her such physical training and exercise as may confirm her health, and perfect her beauty; the highest refinement of that beauty being unattainable without splendour of activity and of delicate strength. (1865: 78)

When it is quoted in isolation, this passage seems to suggest an emphasis on a woman's decorative qualities, but Ruskin continues to assert that it is only with a healthy body that a woman will be able to attain a healthy mind that will enable her to learn. Ruskin's view of women's education is somewhat limited. He understands that women are not yet realizing their potential, but his investment in their fulfilment of it does not reflect a commitment to female education for its own sake, but rather a belief that a well-educated woman will make a better wife.

Religious crises

From this historical remove, the Victorians appear to have been a deeply religious society. However, evidence suggests a somewhat more complicated picture. A census measuring church attendance was taken in March 1851 and revealed that only 50 per cent of the English population had been to a religious service on Sunday, 30 March. Out of these people only half had been worshipping at an Anglican church, suggesting that the nation's official religion was less influential than was previously imagined. On one level these figures point to the growing popularity of 'dissenting' religions (i.e. those which did conform to the doctrines of the Church of England), but the fact that half of the people had not been to church at all is a telling one.

While the Church of England may have been the nation's official religion, dissenting religions including Methodism and Unitarianism were on the rise in the growing manufacturing towns in the North of England, at least partly because of the charitable work their members performed in the industrial slum areas. Dissenting religions that emphasized good works and earthly prosperity as signs of divine grace or election were particularly popular among manufacturers, partly because they seemed to justify the enormous sums of money that were being made through trade. Identifying a convergence between the prevalent Utilitarian doctrine of the 'greatest happiness of the greatest number' and the beliefs of dissenters, Barbara Dennis has commented that for businessmen, 'divine approval could be inferred from the soaring profits' (2000: 27). Attempting to account for the growing numbers of dissenters, Robin Gilmour has noted the diversity of the beliefs and practices of the many nonconformist religions, while also observing the rise of Catholicism in Victorian Britain (1993: 70). The Irish Potato Famine (1845–52) in particular led to a surge in numbers of Roman Catholics, as Irish families sought refuge from starvation by relocating en masse to mainland Britain.

A further explanation for the apparent rise in the influence of dissenting religions stemmed from changes in the law. Legislation in the early decades of the nineteenth century showed a growing tolerance towards other religions, whose practitioners had traditionally been excluded from English civic life. Amendments, including the repeal of the Tests and Corporations Act in 1828 and the Catholic Relief Act of 1829, sought to ease centuries of exclusion and persecution, which although directed towards Catholics had also affected other nonconformists.

Catholicism continued to be a controversial topic for the Victorians even after emancipation, although this was partly a result of centuries of persecution and prejudice. However, the rise of the Tractarian Movement (also known as the Oxford Movement) in the 1830s whipped up anxieties about a popish conspiracy to infiltrate Anglicanism. In July 1833, John Keble gave a sermon that attacked the government's abolition of 22 Irish bishoprics and condemned parliamentary interference in affairs of the Church, arguing that religion should be beyond political influence. This sermon marked the beginning of Tractarianism (named because of the 90 papers comprising *Tracts for the Times* published between 1833 and 1841) under the leadership of Keble, John Henry Newman and Edmund Pusey. The Tractarians stressed the links between the Church of England and Roman Catholicism, arguing for the absolute authority of the Church and a direct line from the Roman Catholicism and Anglicanism. Many of the Tractarians were drawn to the ritual associated with Catholicism and they also rejected the 39 Articles, which were drawn up to differentiate between the Roman Church and the Church of England, arguing that they were little more than a piece of political pragmatism.

While Keble and Pusey ultimately remained within the Church of England as advocates of the highly ritualized 'High Anglicanism', Newman converted to Catholicism in 1845. His actions sent shockwaves through the religious and intellectual community and for a time there were fears that other would follow him over to Rome. Mr Hale in *North and South* seems to have been influenced by

Newman, given that the entire narrative is driven by his inability to confirm his commitment to the 39 Articles. Mr Hale does not take the final step of converting to Catholicism (although, importantly, his exiled son Frederick does when he marries a Spanish Catholic woman), but instead spends the remainder of the novel without any firm affiliation to a Church. His religious beliefs and charitable actions never dwindle; his retreat to the North of England symbolizes the distance he has travelled from Anglicanism.

Evolution and faith

The nineteenth century was punctuated by a number of religious crises, which, like the effects of Tractarianism, were often depicted in realist novels. According to Philip Davis, 'the most powerful religious phenomenon of the [Victorian] age was religious doubt, the sheer life-seriousness with which the threat of unbelief was experienced by those who could live in ease neither with nor without religion' (2004: 101). There were many reasons underlying this doubt. For some, industrialism itself created a sense of nihilism as they struggled to deal with how greatly and rapidly the world was changing. Thomas Hardy registered this shift in his novel *Jude the Obscure* (1895) in which the central female character, Sue Bridehead, would rather sit in the railway station than look at a cathedral. While for freethinking Sue the modernity of the station displaces the Church, for large numbers of Victorians scientific and technological progress were sources of great terror and uncertainty.

Many Victorians experienced a challenge to their faith as they tried to reconcile the unearthing of prehistoric fossils with the word of the Bible. Although not a Victorian publication, Sir Charles Lyell's *Principles of Geology* (1830–33) disrupted belief in the chronology of the creation of the world laid out in the Bible, challenging the idea that the earth was created in six days and making it difficult for scientists to believe in the great flood. The discovery of the remains of a Neanderthal man in Germany in 1857 presented further complications for those who read the Bible literally, in that their great age cast doubt on the established story of creation.

Charles Darwin may have crystallized the evolutionary debate with the publication of *On the Origin of Species* in 1859, yet his work was by no means unanticipated. Eighteenth-century scientists like Jean-Baptiste de la Marck and Erasmus Darwin had paved the way for the evolutionary debates developed in works like Robert Chambers' *Vestiges of the Natural History of Creation* (1844) and *The Origin*. It is therefore important to register that although Darwin is the figure with whom we primarily associate evolution today, his ideas were not unanticipated and were under discussion in well-educated households across the nation in the 1840s and 1850s. Alfred, Lord Tennyson's great poem *In Memoriam* (published in 1850, although Tennyson had begun work on it in 1833) famously explored some of the religious doubts he experienced while thinking through the implications of extinction and what that might mean for humanity.

The angel in the house

The Victorian novel was an important forum for discussing the changing position of women. Although traditionally women had worked alongside their husbands, with the growth of industrial capitalism in the eighteenth century and the vast riches that it yielded for successful entrepreneurs, it became a sign of prosperity to have a leisured wife and daughters. As a result, wealthy women were regularly treated almost as though they were invalids, spending hours languishing in drawing rooms and taking very little exercise.

In the early nineteenth century, Jane Austen offered a number of parodies of the inactive aristocratic woman, most memorably the almost completely inert Lady Bertram in *Mansfield Park* (1814). As the manufacturing classes consolidated their great wealth and began to seek admission to the gentry, middle-class women followed suit. John Thornton's sister Fanny in *North and South* exemplifies such a woman, steeped in boredom and endlessly inventing illnesses in a bid to while away her time. Although she is a much more resourceful young woman, Elizabeth-Jane in *The Mayor of Casterbridge* incurs Henchard's wrath when he learns that she has worked for her keep at a guest house and again when she cannot prevent herself from assisting domestic servants when they appear to need help.

The middle-class woman was an idealized figure, constrained by prescribed modes of conduct and expectations. While women had been important participants in the shift to a capitalist economy, by the middle of the eighteenth century it had become a sign of prosperity to have a leisured wife. As a consequence, women were increasingly identified with the world of the domestic. This division of the world into the public, or male sphere, and the private is known as 'separate spheres ideology', although the term is a little misleading in that it suggests that there was no overlap between the two worlds, when clearly men inhabited the private sphere and women inevitably spent some time in the public realm. Furthermore, this separation is problematic when it is applied to the working-class family, where women often combined their domestic duties with paid work in the very public domain of the factory.

Virginia Woolf has rather cruelly parodied the Victorian 'angel in the house' in a bid to cast off her influence and forge a position for herself as a modern woman:

> She was intensely sympathetic. She was immensely charming. She was utterly unselfish. She excelled in the difficult arts of family life. She sacrificed herself daily. If there was chicken, she took the leg; if there was a draught, she sat in it – in short she was so constituted that she never had a mind or a wish of her own, but preferred to sympathize always with the minds and wishes of others. Above all – I need not say it – she was pure. (1947: 152)

Although highly satirical, Woolf's caricature of Victorian feminine virtues captures the emphasis on self-sacrifice that governed many women's lives in the nineteenth century. Women were regarded as the moral compasses of the family, responsible for instilling morality in their children and for providing a pleasant home environment for their husbands.

Woolf's version of the domestic angel is extreme and it is important to register that many Victorian women were as troubled by this ideal as Woolf herself. Eliot's Maggie Tulliver, for instance, is never able to conform to this model of feminine deportment and is, as a consequence, significantly more engaging than her mother and aunts whose lives revolve around the accumulation of household items like linen and plates. Equally, while Margaret Hale is much more conventional in her conduct than Maggie, the plot of *North and South* is driven by her refusal to be confined to the domestic sphere. As I'll show in Part Two, all of the novels we are considering reveal resistance to the confinement of women to the home. Even the earliest work under discussion, *Oliver Twist,* features a perfect domestic woman in the form of the angelic Rose Maylie. However, her excessive goodness is undermined by the stain of illegitimacy that seems to surround her birth, while it is also offset by her textual doubling with the prostitute Nancy. Far from upholding the angel in the house, then, the Victorian novel sought to challenge and liberate her.

The fin de siècle

Although still part of the Victorian period, the closing decades of the nineteenth century have their own distinct identity and are known as the *fin de siècle*, or the end of the century. The French phrase is used to convey the feelings of exhaustion and acute boredom (also known as 'ennui') that can sometimes mark the end of a long period. The fin de siècle meant different things to different Victorians. For some, it was a time of crisis and anxiety; the Queen, who had been on the throne since 1837 had come to embody the spirit of the age, and it was obvious that she could not go on forever. The Prince of Wales was not regarded as a suitably responsible successor and there were grave concerns about his ability to fill his mother's place. Many late Victorians experienced a feeling of inadequacy or belatedness, believing that the great technological and creative accomplishments of the early and mid-Victorians marked the pinnacle of human achievement and that anything to follow would simply be a pale imitation of what had gone before.

A period of economic depression meant that Britain's status as the 'workshop of the world' was in jeopardy as competitors in Europe and the United States of America with newer, more efficient machinery began to undercut British manufacturing. Meanwhile, Britain expanded her imperial horizons, developing a more coherent colonial policy than ever before, particularly in relation to the so-called Scramble for Africa in which European powers thrashed out their antagonism in Africa, carving the continent into colonial holdings in the process.

For other Victorians, this time of transition was exciting and energizing. It offered the opportunity to overturn some of the stuffiness associated with 'high' Victorianism and to depart from convention. The issues that threatened some Victorians and exhilarated others were often the same ones – while the decadents and New Women revelled in challenges to gender identities, for instance, more conservative figures were aghast. Gail Marshall has commented that the fin de siècle was 'an age conscious of itself as an era of new beginnings, but also one whose movements are defined by the extent to which they developed away from their Victorian roots' (2007: 5). Marshall goes on to suggest that the period was one in which 'debate and controversy are central' (5), which makes it both a fascinating period to study, but also one that is extremely slippery and difficult to pin down. In many respects the fin de siècle is a transitional time, marking the movement between Victorianism and Modernism, yet remaining distinct from both.

The New Woman

Those Victorians who believed that the establishment was under attack were particularly challenged by the figure of the 'New Woman'. The term, 'New Woman' was coined by the novelist and social activist Sarah Grand, writing in 1894, although the label is misleading in that it covered many different types of womanhood and those women identified as 'new' came to prominence from the 1880s onwards. Some of the more visible New Women were political campaigners, who wanted better access to education and, in some cases, the right to vote. It is, of course, wrong to suggest that these concerns emerged suddenly at the end of the nineteenth century. We need only look to Mary Wollestonecraft's *Vindication of the Rights of Woman* (1792) to see that the issue of female emancipation had a much longer history.

It is difficult to identify a single reason behind the rise of the New Woman. The National Society for Women's Suffrage had been formed in 1867 and regularly presented Bills to Parliament, demanding that women be allowed the right to vote. A shortage of men was also a contributing factor, with the 1851 census noting that there were 400,000 more women than men in the country. These women came to be known as 'surplus women' (George Gissing rather cruelly parodied them in his novel of 1893, *The Odd Women*) and their existence posed a direct challenge to the belief that a woman's mission in life was to marry, support her husband and raise children. They were the subject of great debate, with articles like W. R. Greg's 'Why are Women Redundant?' (*National Review*, 1862) and Frances Power Cobbe's 'What Shall We Do with Our Old Maids?' (*Fraser's Magazine*, 1862) examining the vulnerability of the additional women. These 'spare' women could not rely on a husband to keep them and, many needing to earn their own living, they looked to the world of work. Some became teachers or governesses, while towards the end of the century, inventions like the typewriter meant that women could pursue careers as secretaries or journalists. Cobbe went so far as to argue that 'those women who do possess the noble love of knowledge and are willing to undergo the drudgery of its acquirement, should have every aid supplied and every stumbling block removed from their paths' (101).

Given the realist novel's engagement with social and political events in the real world, it is hardly surprising that a new form of fiction, the 'New Woman Novel' emerged. These texts were as varied as the New Women themselves, and according to Talia Schaffer, 'Fictionalizing the New Woman allowed her to be defined in any way the author needed, at any time' (2001: 57). While some New Women opposed marriage, others embraced it; some rejected motherhood outright, while others (particularly those with an understanding of the emerging science of eugenics) favoured the idea of 'civic motherhood', choosing a suitably robust mate in order to breed and to raise a new generation of physically and intellectually vigorous children. These differing agendas did not prevent the press from demonizing the New Woman, presenting her as a danger to herself, to society and to future generations.

The New Women we will meet in these pages are tame by comparison with some 'wild women' who emerged at the end of the nineteenth century. New Woman writers like Sarah Grand tackled unmentionable subjects including syphilis in their fiction, with a view to educating woman readers and helping them to take control of their bodies. *Dracula*'s Mina Harker is, by contrast a mild and compliant woman, who, as I shall discuss in Part Two, does not deliberately pit herself against the mores of her day. Maggie Tulliver in *The Mill on the Floss*, while not a New Woman, demonstrates the need for women to be allowed outlets for their abilities and access to education. Significantly more intelligent than her brother Tom, Maggie's potential is dismissed and even ridiculed because her society cannot contain her, while her agonies and frustrations anticipate a number of the concerns associated with womanhood at the end of the nineteenth century. Noting the connection between Eliot's heroines with their immense, wasted talents, and the more emancipated women of the fin de siècle, Grant Allen invokes George Eliot directly in his scandalous New Woman novel, *The Woman Who Did* (1895), with his heroine Herminia Barton lashing out at Eliot for marrying later in her life. What the impulsive Herminia fails to understand is that Eliot's historical context was even more restrictive than her own. While Herminia was at first willing to conduct an experiment in free love and suffered the consequences when she was left alone with a child, Eliot was not prepared to condemn Maggie Tulliver to a similar fate.

The Dandy and homosexuality at the fin de siècle

Frequently presented as a male counterpart to the New Woman, the Dandy was regarded as equally subversive and just as threatening. While the Dandy was flamboyant in dress and often known for his decadent conduct, he was not always a homosexual, although a number of high-profile dandies were. Nevertheless, he was perceived as a threat to the future of the British race because of his effete manners and alleged self-absorption. Linda Dowling has highlighted the connection between the New Woman and the decadent man, commenting:

> To most late Victorians the decadent was new and the New Woman decadent. The origins, tendencies, even the appearance of the New Woman and the decadent – as portrayed in the popular press and periodicals – confirmed their near, their unhealthily near relationship. Both inspired reactions ranging from hilarity to disgust and outrage, and both raised as well profound fears for the future of sex, class, and race. (1996: 48–9)

The Dandy thus became a focal point for late-Victorian fears surrounding masculinity and the regulation of the male body.

In many respects the Dandy was epitomized by Oscar Wilde, who sought to express his originality through increasingly ostentatious dress, and who became more and more daring in his public and private conduct in the 1890s. Although Wilde was married with two sons, he embarked upon a relationship with Lord Alfred Douglas, the son of the Marquess of Queensbury, for which he was imprisoned in 1895. Legislation against male homosexuality had been introduced as an addendum to the Labouchère Amendment of 1885. This Bill had been introduced to Parliament in a bid to combat an illicit trade in underage female virgins whose life of prostitution was sensationally exposed by W. T. Stead in *The Maiden Tribute of Modern Babylon,* which appeared in the *Pall Mall Gazette* in 1885. Just before the Bill was passed, Henry Labouchère added an ambiguous clause, which was rushed through without debate. Under the Amendment, which came to be known as 'the blackmailer's charter', male homosexuality was essentially rendered illegal. The wording in fact outlawed 'gross indecency', but provided no definition of what that might actually entail. The Amendment, which was not repealed until 1967, was used to prosecute and persecute homosexual men, and Wilde was its first high-profile victim.

Talia Schaffer, in her well-known article 'A Wilde Desire Took Me' (1994), draws an intriguing parallel between the plot of *Dracula* and the Wilde Trials. Noting that Stoker began work on *Dracula* a month after his friend Oscar Wilde was convicted of 'sodomy', Schaffer argues that the novel is an exploration of Stoker's own fears as a repressed or secret homosexual. Schaffer is not the only critic to note *Dracula*'s homoerotic subtext. Christopher Craft is one of several critics to explore Jonathan Harker's 'hysteria', and his potentially closeted sexual identity, in a wonderful essay titled 'Kiss Me with Those Red Lips' (1984). Schaffer, however, is the first critic to consider Stoker's personal connection to Wilde in any depth, noting the deep friendship between the two men (Stoker married Florence Balcombe, a woman whom Wilde had also been wooing, and Schaffer follows the work of Eve Kosofsky Sedgwick in arguing that male desire can be displaced onto a woman) and the ways in which Wilde was expunged from Stoker's life after the trial.

Examining Stoker's correspondence, particularly an exchange with the American poet Walt Whitman, Schaffer charts Stoker's movement from being an 'open member of [the] nascent homosexual culture centred around Whitman' in the 1870s and 1880s, to his public demand for the imprisonment of homosexual writers in 1912 (284). Tracing what she calls the 'textual history of Stoker's repressed sexuality' (285), Schaffer examines the ways in which homoerotic desire and guilt are encoded within the text of *Dracula*. She argues that Stoker channelled his desire for his employer, the charismatic actor Henry Irving, into his creation of the Count, while at the same time publicly agitating for greater state regulation of narrative and its content. As Schaffer notes, 'Stoker identifies with the national anti-Wilde homophobia, partly to disguise his own vulnerability as a gay man, partly because it justifies his belief in the value of the closet, and partly from horror at the monstrous image of Wilde produced by the media' (388). She also highlights the unusual degree of censorship carried out by Count Dracula, who burns books and diaries once he is acquainted with their content. Through a sequence of close readings, some of which I shall examine in Part Two, Schaffer makes the convincing claim that 'Dracula reproduces Wilde in all his apparent monstrosity and evil' in order to negotiate and reconfigure his author's anxieties about their shared gay identities (Schaffer, 1994: 471).

Stoker was certainly not the only writer to have been troubled by the Labouchère Amendment. As Elaine Showalter, among others, has argued, it is possible to read Robert Louis Stevenson's *The Strange Case of Dr. Jekyll and Mr. Hyde* (1886) as a 'fable of fin-de-siècle homosexual panic, the discovery and resistance of the homosexual self' (1992: 107). Downplaying the fact that Jekyll and Hyde are two manifestations of the same person, Showalter argues that the novella depicts a familiar late-Victorian scenario, in which the respectable older gentleman travels to the slum areas of London to solicit the services of a younger man of a lower class. Showalter draws out the novel's blackmail plot and offers an intriguing argument for reading Mr Hyde as a syphilitic degenerate, representing a climate of fear in which some sexual activities had by necessity become illicit.

Atavism and degeneration

One of the nightmares to haunt the late Victorians was the fear of backsliding or, as Tennyson put it in *The Idylls of the King*, 'reeling back into the beast' (1856–85). These fears were partly fuelled by interpretations of Darwin's *On the Origin of Species*, with some commentators believing that if it was possible to evolve from apes, then it was just as feasible for evolution to work backwards, with people degenerating into primates. Scientists, including Max Nordau and Cesare Lombroso, circulated theories of degeneration, biologizing criminal characteristics and writing of the threat posed to society by decadent conduct.

Increased attention to working-class bodies and living conditions heightened fears that Great Britain might be on the brink of decline. Economic depression in the 1870s and 1880s put particular pressure on the working classes, and social reformers stepped up their engagement with the urban poor. Those in particularly dire circumstances – namely those without employment, or those whose income fell below the poverty line – were termed the 'residuum', suggesting that they were a type of human waste. Elaine Showalter has noted that 'This netherworld was seen to live in slums, breeding disease, ignorance, madness, and crime . . . The theory of urban degeneration furthermore held that poverty led to a general deterioration of the race' (5). These most desperate members of the underclass were not a new phenomenon – they are visible in Dickens' earliest fiction and, for our purposes, they are embodied by the gang of young thieves who are only able to find a nurturing community through their relationship with the arch-villain, Fagin. By the end of the nineteenth century, though, they had become a much more prominent concern and the area that attracted the most public attention was the East End of London.

While William Blake had long before figured London as a city of the damned in his poem 'London' from the *Songs of Experience* (1794), by the end of the nineteenth century it was perceived as an inferno. The city's East End had always been a problem area, but now it was regarded as a hot bed of disease and crime, which was in danger of spilling out into the wider city. Conditions in the East End were horrific: four out of five working-class families lived in one room, and 55 per cent of children born in the area died before they reached 5 years of age. Those with employment often worked as 'sweated labour', putting in long hours for a minimal wage, while General William Booth, the founder of the Salvation Army, reported that 30 per cent of Londoners were living below the subsistence level.

Britain's involvement in the two Boer Wars (1880–1881 and 1899–1902) also drew attention to the working-class body when it was discovered that 60 per cent of the men who enlisted to fight against the Boers were physically unfit to do so as they were suffering from conditions caused by malnutrition, including scurvy and rickets. Robert Baden-Powell, in direct response to his experiences of fighting in the Transvaal in the second Boer campaign, founded the Boy Scouts in 1908 in a bid to instil discipline and physical vigour into working-class boys. His manual *Scouting for Boys: A Handbook for Instruction in Good Citizenship* has become an important source document for literary and historical scholars with interests in boyhood at the end of the nineteenth century.

In terms of the physical and moral health of the population as a whole, middle-class writers and philanthropists became extremely interested in the East End and a number of novels appeared, drawing attention to the area's terrible otherness. William Booth's *In Darkest England and the Way Out* (1890), George Gissing's *The Nether World* (1889), Arthur Morrison's *A Child of the Jago* (1896) and Margaret Harkness' *In Darkest London* (1889) are just a handful of the novels that drew connections between the slums of London and darkest Africa and adopted a sequence of metaphors suggesting the need for missionary activity at the very heart of the empire. Writers were stimulated by the degradation and horror that they encountered in the capital city, representing the East End as a dangerous labyrinth and pandering to their readers' horrified voyeurism. Many engaged in so-called slumming expeditions, donning disguises and mingling with the underclass, sometimes for philanthropic reasons and sometimes out of curiosity.

The Whitechapel murders and the Nemesis of Neglect

One of the reasons for the growing interest in the living conditions of society's poorest members was a sequence of crimes that continues to intrigue and perplex scholars, detectives and the general public to this day. Between 31 August and 9 November 1888, five murders of prostitutes took place, mainly in the Whitechapel area of East London. The perpetrator was never found and over the years a number of high-profile men have been nominated as potential suspects. So brutal were the slayings that the perpetrator came to be known as 'Jack the Ripper', a name that first appeared in a sequence of letters to the press by someone claiming to be the murderer.

The case became a source of fascination to the newspaper-reading public, and while journalists received more than three hundred letters from people claiming to have insights into the atrocities, the most famous were the 'Ripper' letters, which were addressed to 'Dear Boss' and signed 'From Hell'. Mark Seltzer has argued that the Ripper case saw the beginning of a new approach to both committing and reporting murder, reading a connection between the serial killings and the serialization of the 'story' in the newspapers. He comments, 'Letters and bodies, word counts and body counts, go together from the inception of serial murder' (1998: 9).

Given Whitechapel's proximity to the financial district of London, the Ripper murders turned the public's attention to the troubled East End. Metaphors of contamination abounded as people began to realize that crime and disease could not be contained in the slums of London indefinitely. As panic spread, so too did the fear that London was in the grip of a crime epidemic In a famous cartoon entitled 'The Nemesis of Neglect' the well-known satirical journal *Punch* illustrated how society's unwillingness to improve slum areas like the East End was responsible for crime and other social evils. The idea of the Ripper as a 'nemesis' suggests that his actions constituted a type of justice or retribution for the way society had failed the East Enders.

Jack the Ripper became a kind of blank space onto which the newspaper-reading public could offload their darkest fears about the East End of London. The faceless killer came to embody the barbarism that many associated with London's underclass, and the social groupings of the immediate suspects point to a number of late-Victorian class and racial tensions. Although there were no witnesses to any of the crimes, some believed that a 'gentleman' or aristocrat was responsible, while others attempted to pin the murders on the recent wave of Eastern European Jews who had fled persecution to settle in the East End. As Seth Koven notes in his extended study of 'slumming', 'the Jack the Ripper murders made Whitechapel the epicentre of elite fantasies about sexual and social disorder' (2004: 128), but for many it also became a locus for their worst nightmares.

Bram Stoker certainly responded to the hype surrounding the Jack the Ripper murders when he wrote *Dracula*, which appeared nine years after the killing spree. The Count is both an aristocrat and, as critics including Jules Zanger and Christopher Herbert have noted – as I shall briefly discuss in Part Three – he also possesses a number of Semitic characteristics that point to late nineteenth-century concerns about immigration. The reporting of the Count's crimes follows the type of serialization that characterized the Ripper reports, with the journalist latching onto catchy names, as when he transforms Lucy Westenra into the 'bloofer lady', providing a subtle parallel between the bloodthirsty Count and the killer who had terrorized London. Moreover, while on some levels he may be considered a type of supernatural master criminal, on others Dracula appears to be an atavistic throwback, with a 'child's brain' and a gruesome appetite for the blood of others. With his imperialistic desire to invade England and populate it with the un-dead, Dracula embodies the late-Victorian fear both of the unstoppable killer who resists detection and the degenerate who seeks to spread his contamination across the nation.

The Empire

The publication of Edward Said's now classic study, *Orientalism*, in 1978 has resulted in a heightened attention to the colonial plots, subplots and backdrops featured in nineteenth-century novels. With improvements in transportation and schemes to encourage relocation, such as Caroline Chisholm's famous 'Family Colonization Loan Society', designed to help thrifty working-class people to relocate abroad, Britain's imperial holdings were an increasingly important destination. While some travelled to the Empire for adventures, others saw trading opportunities and still others saw the possibility of beginning a new life on the other side of the world. The Empire became a highly important plot device, although given the growing importance of the colonies to everyday life, it is inevitable that the realist novel would concern itself with imperial issues.

In a lecture in 1883 the historian Sir John Seeley notoriously quipped 'We seem, as it were, to have conquered and peopled half the world in a fit of absence of mind' (10). While Seeley's comments made light of Britain's rapid accumulation of territory in the closing decades of the nineteenth century, they highlighted the somewhat haphazard acquisition of colonial holdings across the globe. At the end of the century, as Britain was drawn into the Scramble for Africa by rogue entrepreneurs like Cecil Rhodes, the Empire expanded to incorporate 4.5 million square miles of land and 66 million people (Boehmer, 1995: 31).

The British Empire, in spite of its magnitude, was not the result of a sustained policy of imperial growth and occupation. As Lance Davis and Robert Huttenback have pointed out, territory was often acquired in order to protect the trading interests of private British companies (1986: 137). India, for instance, was not formally incorporated into the British Empire until the 1857 Indian 'mutiny' (today known as the First Indian War of Independence) had been put down. The British, though, had been trading in India since the reign of Elizabeth I, and the British East India Company (founded in 1708 as a result of the merger of two rival businesses) gradually mutated from a private concern (it lost its trade monopoly in 1813) to a British government agency after 1834. Although originally a business, the Company ruled India in the first half of the nineteenth century, but was hastily dismantled following allegations, including widespread torture and general mismanagement, which emerged in the aftermath of the 'mutiny'.

India played a significant role in the Victorian novel, particularly after 1851 when a spectacularly exotic display at the Great Exhibition in the Crystal Palace captured the public imagination. I don't want to suggest that readers suddenly 'discovered' India at this point, after all writers, including the Indian-born William Makepeace Thackeray and Charlotte Brontë, had drawn on Indian subplots in their novels, and Philip Meadows Taylor's *Confessions of a Thug* (1839) had attracted enormous interest. Furthermore, many readers would already have been familiar with the calls for reform in India from the prolific social theorist Harriet Martineau and others who shared her concerns at how the East India Company was managing India. Nevertheless, after 1851 the reading public showed an immense appetite for writings about India, Wilkie Collin's detective novel *The Moonstone* (1868) offering one particularly famous example.

In 1877 Queen Victoria was crowned Empress of India, having been persuaded by the Prime Minister, Benjamin Disraeli, to adopt the title. Disraeli was an astute political operator, who understood the role that the Empire could play in unifying the British people. By celebrating Britain's exploits overseas and encouraging patriotism and pride, Disraeli was able to foster a spirit of jingoism and to divert attention from class and economic tensions closer to home. As a consequence, the closing years of the century were marked by a heightened attention to the Empire, both in fiction and in popular culture, with the Queen's Golden Jubilee (1887) and Diamond Jubilee (1897) incorporating considerable displays of imperial strength and pageantry. Stories of colonial adventure by the likes of Rudyard Kipling, G. A. Henty and Henry Rider Haggard became bestsellers, and while the two Boer Wars (1880–1881 and 1899–1902) undermined British assertions of imperial supremacy, on the whole the rhetoric of imperial dominance remained buoyant.

CHAPTER TWO

Literary context

The form of the novel

While we may think about the writings of the period as lengthy tomes, in fact and as the remarks from George Levine quoted in the introduction suggest, Victorian novels came in all shapes and sizes. The form underwent a remarkable sequence of changes over the decades, responding to shifts in readership, developments in print technology and the manufacturing of cheap paper. In the early years of Victoria's reign, those with the leisure to read enjoyed three-volume works, known as triple deckers. The form of these works was partly dictated by Mudie's Circulating Library, an institution that allowed subscribers to borrow an unlimited number of books for the cost of a guinea per year at a time when books were beyond the reach of all but the wealthiest. Mudie's became enormously popular with the leisured classes and, as consequence, Charles Mudie, the founder, became a very powerful figure, able to exclude those authors from his library who did not conform to his views on appropriate moral content. As George Levine notes, Mudie became so influential because his bulk orders meant that publishers were guaranteed a profit on any book he adopted. Mudie favoured the three-volume work because the different parts could be divided between different subscribers so that one book could be shared among three different readers. Appearing on Mudie's list was a guarantee of success for any author, so most writers and publishers attempted to conform to his standards.

Simon Eliot points out that fiction targeted towards working-class readers appeared either in instalments or a single volume (2001: 41) and indeed, when Dickens commenced his career, he was repeatedly warned against publishing in parts, lest he be considered a 'lowbrow' author as a consequence. In fact, so great was Dickens' influence, that he contributed to the increased respectability of the serial form.

Literacy rates had risen throughout Victoria's reign, although as Richard D. Altick notes, they are extremely difficult to quantify as they tended to be measured by people's ability to write their own names (1973: 60). The growth of institutions like the Manchester Working Men's College and the Manchester Mechanics' Institute, founded to promote the education of working men, along with the development of cheap printing techniques, which enabled the mass production of novels, increasing numbers of working men and women were able to enjoy novels when they had the time. Furthermore, anecdotal evidence about Charles Dickens' popularity suggests that even the illiterate had access to fiction, and there are stories of working people pooling their money to buy the next instalment of a novel like *The Pickwick Papers* for a designated reader to read aloud. Dickens took this idea one step further towards the end of his life, when he embarked upon a number of highly popular reading tours, adapting his most popular works and performing to great acclaim.

By the end of the century, novelists including George Moore, Thomas Hardy and George Gissing began to struggle against Mudie's control over the shape and content of the novel, with Moore engaging in a public attack on Mudie through his pamphlet, *Literature at Nurse, or Circulating Morals* in 1885 (41). Gradually, novels began to shorten, partly because public libraries began to challenge Mudie's dominance, but also because of the increased popularity of rail travel. As Simon Eliot reports, in the 1850s and 1860s, publishers (including the hugely influential WH Smith) responded to the new market of railway readers by producing cheap, light volumes for readers on train journeys. Known as 'yellowbacks' or 'railway novels', these books were designed to be portable and while many 'respectable' novels were published in this format, so too were lighter works, including sensation fiction and the emerging genre of the detective novel (51–2).

The working classes became increasingly important in determining the novel's shape in the final decades of Victoria's reign, with an estimated 96 per cent of the population being able to read by the beginning of the twentieth century (see Weedon, 2003: 33).

Debates about the quality of reading matter available to working readers surfaced repeatedly throughout the nineteenth century, with objections to the salacious 'penny dreadfuls' of the early to mid-Victorian period shifting into disapproval of the 'shilling shockers' which had replaced them by the end of the century. Increasingly though, as the working classes obtained better education and more leisure time, many novelists shifted their attention to this expanding market. Cheap fiction appeared in single volumes, designed to appeal to the reader who desired something he or she could read quickly and easily after a day of work. As a consequence, detective stories and tales of adventure (particularly those set in the Empire, like H. Rider Haggard's thrilling tales) became extremely popular. Periodical publication continued, but emerging journals like George Newnes' *The Strand Magazine* (started in 1891) gauged their tone to appeal to this new group of readers, with Newnes benefiting particularly from the publication of Conan Doyle's highly popular Sherlock Holmes stories.

The Bildungsroman

Roughly translated from the German as a 'novel of education' or a 'novel of development', the Bildungsroman was a highly popular form during the Victorian period. Given the Victorians' keen interest in the progress of self-made men and the popularity of self-improvement manuals exemplified by Samuel Smiles' famous *Self-Help: With Illustrations of Character and Conduct* (1859), it is hardly a surprise to learn that the Victorians' interest in personal progress extended to their literary taste. Middle-class readers seem to have enjoyed reading about characters battling against the challenges of life and arriving at success by drawing upon their own initiative and resources. Such stories struck a cord with those who had not been born into a life of privilege, but had worked hard to rise to the top.

According to Franco Moretti in *The Way of the World*, the origins of the Bildungsroman may be found in the work of Goethe and Jane Austen (Moretti, 1987: 12), while in France Stendhal developed the genre to draw parallels between the growth of the individual and the development of society. Stendhal's approach is exemplified in his novel *The Red and the Black* (1830), where the protagonist Julien Sorel's progress and decline are aligned with the fortunes of the monarchy during the French Restoration. The English version of the Bildungsroman is, I would argue, more tightly focused around an individual's progress than its European counterpart. Moretti credits George Eliot with continuing to refine the Bildungsroman in English literature, but with the exception of Stoker, all of the novelists represented in this book engaged with the form in some way.

A Bildungsroman often, but not always, begins with a character's birth or early life – Dickens gently parodies this trend in *David Copperfield* with its famous opening, 'Chapter One, I am born', which humorously registers the Bildungsroman's propensity to assemble every little detail of a character's growth. The form goes on to show the character developing and learning, often making mistakes along the way and perhaps being subjected to bad influences or moral danger. Usually the character is cast out into the world through leaving or being forced to leave home. Oliver Twist, Jane Eyre and Margaret Hale all undergo this type of experience, while Maggie Tulliver and Elizabeth-Jane Newson also face similar trials. The character gradually learns through her or his experiences, arriving at adulthood and at some form of success, whether it be fame, marriage (usually the crowning achievement of a female character, rather than a male) or a more general form of moral maturity and acceptance.

Realism

The nineteenth century is often referred to as the great age of realism. Novelists including Charles Dickens, George Eliot and Elizabeth Gaskell responded to the extraordinary changes brought about by industrialism by depicting their effects in their novels as realistically as they could. This is partly because the novelists shared a commitment to social reform and scrutiny of the present, but it is also because of a shared aesthetic through which they sought to create a narrative world that was plausible to the reader, populated by characters with whom he or she could empathize or identify.

George Eliot's relationship with realism was particularly self-reflective, and in her novel *Adam Bede* (1859) Eliot's narrator speaks of her work as 'a faithful account of men and things, as they have mirrored themselves in my mind' (177). Eliot's version of realism sought to be so true to life that although she admitted the subjective nature of her viewpoint, her narrator, in the same passage, continued, 'I feel as much bound to tell you as precisely as I can what that reflection is, as if I were in the witness-box, narrating my experience on oath' (25). While Eliot views realist writing as a responsibility, Dickens' approach differs in early novels like *Oliver Twist*, which combine comedy and realism. As a result characters like Bill Sikes seem absolutely real and utterly terrifying, while they are offset by lighter figures such as the slightly absurd Mr Grimwig, who is constantly threatening to eat his own head. Both Dickens and Eliot use realism as a way of narrating and negotiating a world that is in a state of dynamic and, at times, frightening change. It is therefore important, as we examine the uses and constraints of realist writing, to keep in mind just how closely the Victorian novel was tied to events and changes in the real world.

The realist novel sought to explore what Thomas Carlyle famously termed the 'Condition of England Question', examining some of the challenges thrown up by industrialism, including urban poverty, sanitation, disease and class tensions (Carlyle, 1980: 151). Those who wrote such novels knew that they weren't able to solve these problems, but hoped to focus attention on them through their writing. Victorian realist fiction is generally more democratic than the eighteenth-century novel, which tended to focus on the lives of the very affluent. Following the lead of the Romantic poets in depicting the lives of ordinary people, realist writers like Dickens and Gaskell drew attention to the working men and women who populated the growing cities, while George Eliot and Thomas Hardy are among those who concentrated on rural communities and the difficulties they experienced in the face of industrialism. Terry Eagleton reminds us, 'Dickens's London was a commercial rather than industrial metropolis, which is why the focus of his fictional attention is clerks, lawyers and bankers rather than industrial workers or manufacturers' (2005: 143). Eagleton points out that Dickens was completely ineffective when it came to depicting a manufacturing city; his only industrial novel, *Hard Times*, does not offer an extensive engagement with factory life, nor with Northern culture. Furthermore, Eagleton also alerts us to just how removed Dickens was, as a quintessentially metropolitan writer, from the rural settings of novelists like George Eliot. We therefore need to keep in mind just how diverse the living conditions of these major Victorian novelists were and how these differences impacted upon the form and content of their novels.

There are inevitably tensions between what is actually real and what happens in a realist work. A novel must have a beginning, a middle and – in the Victorian context at least – it must provide adequate resolution and closure so that the reader is satisfied. Pam Morris has argued that there is a 'sense of doubt and ambivalence' underlying English literary realism, continuing to suggest an uncertainty about whether realist writing is really able to convey an accurate sense of reality (2003: 80). Following George Levine, Morris suggests that Victorian writers understood the tensions between the fabricated words on the page and the real world that they claimed to be depicting. For a novelist like Dickens this tension presented interesting creative possibilities, which he explored in some of his later novels, such as *A Tale of Two Cities* and *Great Expectations*. In both of these novels he combined religious symbolism with realist writing to create what Chris Brooks has termed a symbolic realist mode, which could be read and interpreted as both real but also loaded with hidden meanings (see Brooks, 1984).

In trying to move itself beyond the constraints of language, Morris suggests that the Victorian novel also pushes the boundaries of what is considered to be 'normal', taking in elements of the supernatural and the Gothic (2003: 81). This is certainly true of Charlotte Brontë's writing, which uses labyrinthine Gothic imagery to explore many of her characters' psychological states and which pushes the bounds of our credulity by bringing in devices like telepathy or characters like Rochester's 'mad' wife, Bertha Mason. As Morris expresses it, '[t]his vein of otherness and madness undoubtedly contributes powerfully to the ambivalent and multiple sense of reality' (81). However, she also points out that the slippage between realist writing and the real allowed for the rise of the type of interesting, engaging and capable female characters we will meet in the novels we are considering in this book, at a time when the education and conduct of women was often shown to be lacking. Realism had its flaws and shortcomings, then, but Victorian novelists often negotiated them in thoughtfully creative ways.

The problem of ending

Appealing though writing the real might seem, it caused a number of problems for novelists, many of whom began to struggle against some of its perceived constraints. Perhaps the most difficult aspect of realist writing was the tension between the need to provide a realistic conclusion to a novel and the reading public's demand for a 'happy ending'. Deirdre David has suggested that Dickens, Gaskell and Eliot all engaged in creating 'fictions of resolution for the problems of pervasive social uneasiness with which they engage' (1981: x), by which she means that the closure they provide is necessarily contrived. As realist writers these novelists could not simply sweep social problems under the carpet, nor could they bring them to an artificial form of resolution that would be implausible to readers. They therefore had to come up with creative coping strategies that would allow them to end their novels and provide a satisfying ending for the reading public. Thus, mid-Victorian novels frequently close with the central character inheriting money, marrying, emigrating or dying, even though three out of these four plot devices would signal a new beginning rather than an end in real life.

Elizabeth Gaskell worked comfortably within these restrictions, happily marrying Margaret Hale to Mr Thornton at the end of *North and South* or moving her troublesome eponymous heroine Mary Barton to Canada at the end of her 1848 novel. Equally, although he was later to reveal a complex relationship with closure in his last completed work, *Our Mutual Friend*, Dickens was still finding his feet as a realist novelist in *Oliver Twist*. Inflected by the eighteenth-century novel, Oliver's story combines comedy and gothic horror and is conservative in the conclusion it offers, with the implausibly good Oliver finding sanctuary in a middle-class home and being restored to his family. In his later works, however, Dickens registered and reacted against the triteness that can ensue when an author attempts to pull too many narrative threads together and to force too many happy endings. As I shall explore in Part Two, however, both Charlotte Brontë and George Eliot worked against these neat forms of closure that sought to elide the many difficulties of life in the nineteenth century, particularly the lives of women.

The flight from the real

Bram Stoker's *Dracula* may seem to sit somewhat strangely alongside the other more conventionally realist novels under discussion here. However, I have chosen Stoker's popular vampire tale deliberately as a somewhat extreme example of how some novelists chose to push the boundaries of realism. I don't want to suggest that somehow realist writing ceased to exist at the end of the nineteenth century, as it certainly did not. Indeed, a novelist like Henry James, with his deep fascination for the workings of the human mind, offers an excellent example of the ways in which serious-minded writers continued to extend the possibilities that realist writing offered for exploring individual characters and their psychological complexities.

Dracula has been a latecomer to literary studies, having been dismissed for many years as a piece of late-Victorian pulp. However, renewed interest in the distinctness of the writing that appeared at the end of the nineteenth century, along with the establishment of cultural studies as an academic discipline, has meant that *Dracula* is now regarded as a novel that can command serious scholarly attention. By the closing years of the nineteenth century a number of novelists had moved away from the mid-Victorian impulse to structure fiction around social problems and were instead exploring the limits of fantasy. As I mentioned in Chapter One, this was partly a response to a new readership, but also a recognition of the growing importance of science and technology and a reaction to the uncertainties that lay ahead in the twentieth century. Aware of the possibilities for progress in the new century, writers like H. G. Wells, the author of *The Time Machine* (1895) and *The War of the Worlds* (1898), produced what we would today term 'speculative fiction', which appealed to the mass readership because of its riveting adventure plots.

Dracula is part of a late nineteenth-century Gothic revival and although it contains elements of realist writing – for instance the journals, newspaper reports and letters of which the novel is comprised – it also resists many of the restrictions associated with representing the real. To begin with, the vampire himself is clearly not a character we would expect to meet in everyday life. Stoker was not the inventor of the vampire story – the vampire myth itself was centuries old – but the scale of the Count's attack is both ambitious and sensational in its proportions. Far from preying on a few people as other literary vampires had done, Dracula threatens the whole of British society. Stoker's aim here is clearly to create a being who is utterly terrifying and, in so doing, he seeks to appeal to the new generation of working-class readers who, it was believed, demanded reading matter that was both salacious and un-taxing.

Dracula is less concerned with character than most realist novels and the exciting fast-paced plot is of considerably more importance than any of the individuals we encounter. Compared with the protagonists of any of the other five novels we will explore in this guide, *Dracula*'s characters are scantily drawn and lacking in psychological depth. While in a realist novel character is of paramount importance, in *Dracula* it is the action and the Count's curious magnetism that are central. We do gain some insights into the characters and their motivations, primarily through their diary entries, but the novel's shorter length means that characters are not able to unfold to the same degree as they were in a triple-decker novel. Nevertheless, the story has continued to delight readers for more than a century, at least partly because of its obvious difference from the didacticism of the mid-Victorian novel, and because of the ways it resists the conventions and constraints of realist fiction.

Realism continued to flourish in some quarters at the century's end, in spite of its rejection by novelists like Stoker. English novelists including George Gissing and H. G. Wells were increasingly influenced by Emile Zola's Naturalist writing, which aimed to provide a more scientific approach to character, and which made the realist novel 'grittier' than it had been in the mid-Victorian period. Naturalism was a literary response to evolutionary theory and an increased understanding of genetics. The Naturalist novelist adopted the position of a scientist, experimenting on his characters from a distance and attempting to avoid lengthy intrusions from an omniscient narrator. Rather than being the victims of fate, characters were set up with inherited traits, such as a propensity to alcoholism or crime, and they were sometimes given physical disabilities to add to their tribulations. Instead of offering judgements on characters, as the narrator of a realist novel might, the narrative voice in a Naturalist novel sought to appear as objective and rational, leaving the characters to create their own impressions on readers.

Although, as Suzanne J. Flynn reminds us, Thomas Hardy was uncomfortable at being aligned with the Naturalist school, the trials to which he subjects his characters, who are often, as in the case of Michael Henchard, stricken with inherited vices, suggest that his work was more influenced by this style of writing than he was prepared to register (Flynn, 2010: 92). Regardless of any formal association Hardy was, like Stoker, a novelist in transition, positioned between the Victorian and the modern and reflecting qualities of the old and the new worlds in his writing.

Review

- The Victorian period was a time of fast and unprecedented change.
- It is extremely difficult to generalize about Victorian culture or the Victorian novel, partly because of the length of Queen Victoria's reign (1837–1901) and partly because of the many developments in publishing technology and literacy.
- The Victorian novel responded to a range of social, economic and political changes, including the rise to power of the middle class, the movement of the population from rural to metropolitan dwellings, the question of women's education and their role in society.
- Victorian novelists experienced a tension between the demands of realist writing and the need to provide their works with satisfactory conclusions.
- Realist writing attempted to deal with the rapid pace of change and became a form in which social reform could be discussed, as is exemplified by the rise of the 'industrial novel' in the 1840s and 1850s and the increased attention to women's issues in the final decades of the nineteenth century.
- The Victorian novel changed its form as it responded to changes in readership (e.g. the rise of working-class readers after Forster's Education Act in 1870), moving from the lengthy 'triple-decker' tome, which appeared in three volumes, to a shorter single volume by the end of the century. These shorter volumes appealed to working readers, but also sparked concerns about the quality of both content and writing.

Reading

- Deirdre David (ed.), *The Cambridge Companion to the Victorian Novel* (2001)
- Pamela K. Gilbert, *Cholera and Nation: Doctoring the Social Body in Victorian England* (2008)
- Robin Gilmour, *The Victorian Period: The Intellectual and Cultural Context of English Literature, 1830–1890* (1994)
- Sally Ledger, *The New Woman: Fiction and Feminism at the Fin de Siècle* (1997)
- Sally Mitchell, *Daily Life in Victorian England* (1996)
- Maureen Moran, *Victorian Literature and Culture* (2006)
- Pam Morris, *Realism* (2003)
- Alexis Weedon, *Victorian Publishing: The Economics of Book Production for a Mass Market, 1836–1916* (2003)
- Michael Wheeler, *English Fiction of the Victorian Period, 1830–1890* (1994)

Research

- Think about how your experience of reading a novel differs from that of the Victorians. Go back to one of the novels that was published in parts (*Oliver Twist*, *North and South*) and look at how the need to retain readerly interest shapes the narrative. Pay particular attention to the transitions between chapters and the author's use of devices like the 'cliffhanger'.
- Consider some of the characteristics of realist writing. Looking at one of the novels we are discussing in this guide, think about any tensions you might detect between its representation of the real and its author's use of other genres. Is there, for example, a difficulty in combining realism and humour, as Dickens does in *Oliver Twist*?
- Consider Dickens' representation of London in *Oliver Twist* and compare it with Gaskell's portrait of Milton-Northern in *North and South*. How does the capital city compare

with the industrial region? You might pay attention to issues including pollution, life on the street, the character of the city-dweller, class tensions and work. How is London, as a financial centre, different from the northern industrial city? You might also think about how Gaskell's characters engage with London and at times dismiss the southern city as irrelevant.

- Mark Knight and Emma Mason have commented, 'Religion was not just another aspect of the nineteenth century: it found its way into every area of life, from family to politics, sport to work, church architecture to philanthropy' (2006: 9). Think about how religion permeates some of the Victorian novels you have encountered. Do you see religion guiding characters' choices, or do you find its omission curious? Does the author draw on religious symbolism or imagery and if so, to what effect?
- Looking at one mid- and one late-Victorian novel, pay attention to how the representation of women changes towards the end of the nineteenth century. You might, for example, compare Lucy Westenra in *Dracula* with Margaret Hale from *North and South*. Think about how each woman articulates (or fails to articulate) her desires, pay attention to their interactions with male characters and consider the degree to which women have been emancipated in the 42 years between the two texts.

PART TWO

Texts

CHAPTER THREE

Readings of key texts

Oliver Twist, the unprotected child

Charles Dickens frequently used his novels as a means of highlighting the need for social reform and *Oliver Twist* was written as a direct response to the Poor Law Amendment Act. Having himself experienced poverty as a child, including a brief, but traumatic period working at Warren's Blacking Factory while his father was imprisoned for debt, Dickens understood what it meant to be poor and vulnerable. In writing *Oliver Twist* he aimed to expose the living conditions of the poorest members of society, focusing particularly on the vulnerability of children and the way in which poverty and desperation led the young to a life of crime. Knowing that his middle-class readers would be horrified by the uncouth conduct of a genuine street child, Dickens transplanted the sensitive, genteel *Oliver Twist* into a world of vice, penury and crime. From a realist perspective, one of the novel's flaws is that in spite of being raised in a workhouse among paupers, Oliver's speech is distinctly middle-class and his conduct is implausibly virtuous. When he is unable to contend with the horror of a situation, he swoons, and thus avoids it, whereas a genuine street urchin would have to have been much more robust in order to survive.

The workhouse is represented as a world of total isolation and the early chapters emphasize Oliver's loneliness. Laura Peters has noted that Oliver is repeatedly orphaned; that his parentless state is reinforced by the institutions that are supposed to be caring for him, which instead of acting as substitutes for the parents he has never known, simply emphasize his isolation and accentuate his orphaned state (2001: 37). Dickens draws our attention to the state's failings when he describes Oliver as 'a parish child – the orphan of a workhouse – the humble half-starved drudge – to be cuffed and buffeted through the world – despised by all, and pitied by none' (3). Dickens also highlights the precariousness of Oliver's position through a series of cannibal motifs that pervade the novel. Boys in the workhouse are described as being so hungry that they wish to eat Oliver, while the slightly ridiculous Mr Grimwig is, as I noted earlier, constantly threatening to eat his own head. Importantly, the austerity of the workhouse is pitted against the more comfortable environment of Fagin's lair. While the workhouse inmates are always hungry, Fagin's boys are well fed and, comparatively speaking, well cared for. Dickens' point here is surely that while Fagin may be a devious criminal, his world is in many ways much more humane than that of the workhouse, suggesting that there are few incentives for the very poor to abide by the laws.

Combining comedy with realism, Dickens allows his readers to enter into the world of poverty, but always mediates their experiences through the eyes of a naïve middle-class child, rather than a more authentic Victorian street urchin. The incongruity between Oliver and his environment is particularly apparent when the orphan summons the courage to leave the workhouse to travel to London by himself. Although small and weak, he decides that he will walk 70 miles and we learn that he is, quite miraculously, able to cover 20 miles in one day. Unlikely though some of Oliver's physical accomplishments may seem, Dickens still manages to evoke sympathy for his character, drawing attention to his frailty and the sheer terror of being a child, alone in the world: 'His feet were sore, and his legs so weak that they trembled beneath him. Another night passed in the bleak damp air, made him worse; when he set forward on his journey next morning, he could hardly crawl along' (51). The scene continues with the narrator's account of the suspicion Oliver meets, wherever he goes:

> In some villages, large painted boards were fixed up: warning all persons who begged within the district, that they would be sent to jail. This frightened Oliver very much, and made him glad to get out of those villages with all possible expedition. In others, he

> would stand about the inn-yards, and look mournfully at every one who passed; a proceeding which generally terminated in the landlady's ordering one of the post-boys who were lounging about, to drive that strange boy out of the place, for she was sure he had come to steal something. (51)

This account vividly conveys how nineteenth-century society has criminalized poverty, even within the very young. The large boards reveal that the legal system has quashed compassion, with the suggestion that anyone, regardless of circumstances, will be punished for trying to survive if they resort to the demeaning act of begging. The signs represent a blanket enforcement of the law, with no attempt to understand the circumstances that might have given rise to the desperate act. Furthermore, the landlady's assumption that Oliver must be a criminal is at odds with what we have previously learned about the beauty and innocence of the young boy's face. Oliver's poverty effaces the visible signifiers of his good breeding and moral rectitude, so that those he meets on the way to London are unable to see beyond the beggar.

Gaskell, the working poor and the lady visitor

While *Oliver Twist* explores the criminal underworld as a way of examining urban poverty and providing a critique of existing welfare provisions, Elizabeth Gaskell's *North and South* is much more concerned with the working poor and their living conditions. Like Dickens, Gaskell uses the device of placing a genteel character in a working-class world so that her readers are not completely overwhelmed and alienated by her portrait of an industrial city. *North and South* is a novel of reconciliation and adaptability, in which Gaskell attempts to bridge the gaps between the North and the South, the rich and the poor, the masters and the workers. As an educated, well-bred woman, reduced to conditions of genteel poverty, Margaret Hale is ideally situated to mediate between these different worlds.

In economic and social terms, Margaret moves from the centre of society to its margins. The fact that she is clearly a southerner and has obviously been used to a more comfortable standard of living means that she cannot be neatly assimilated into the northern working class and, as I shall discuss in more detail in the section on 'class', she remains separate from those around her. Pamela Corpron Parker has noted that Margaret maintains an anomalous position in relation to the impoverished factory workers that stems from her identity as a parson's daughter, accustomed to visiting the sick and needy. As a minister's wife, Elizabeth Gaskell regularly undertook charitable visits to her husband's parishioners, positioning herself as a genteel philanthropist (Corpron Parker, 1997: 322). Household visiting was a responsibility enthusiastically embraced by a large number of well-intentioned upper- and middle-class women, who wanted to make a difference to the community. Indeed, *The Englishwoman's Yearbook* reported that as many as five hundred thousand women were engaged in philanthropic acts of this kind in 1893 (322).

While for some, the lady visitor was a welcome figure, spreading the gospel and distributing aid in the forms of food or money, for others she was little more than a patronizing nuisance. Dickens famously parodied the forceful, undaunted philanthropist in *Bleak House*'s Mrs Pardiggle, who invades the homes of the poor with her terrifying brand of religion. In *North and South* Margaret's friendship with the Higgins family demonstrates the potentially fraught nature of the unsolicited visit from the lady philanthropist. Without considering the possible distinctions between Northern and Southern etiquette, and forgetting her own newly reduced circumstances, Margaret casually invites herself to visit the invalid Bessy Higgins. While her proposed visit would be considered the norm in her father's rural parish in the South of England, Bessy's father initially regards the suggestion as an unwelcome imposition, responding, 'I'm none so fond of having strange folk in my house' (74). Higgins relents almost immediately, however, demonstrating a sensitivity to Margaret as one whom he terms a 'foreigner' in recognition of her cultural difference.

Margaret's excursions take her far beyond her usual sphere, into the public streets, where her presence raises interesting questions about gender, class and the politics of space. While her family is poor, Margaret has been raised in the household of her wealthy aunt and is accustomed to a life of privilege. Having acted as a type of companion to her spoiled cousin, Edith, Margaret returns to her parents when Edith is married. Although they have little material wealth, Margaret's father's position as a clergyman allows him some status and respect within the community. When the change in his beliefs forces him to leave the Church, Mr Hale still commands some esteem, since he has been educated and has the manners of a gentleman. A number of other characters express confusion at the Hales' circumstances, finding it difficult to 'place' these people whose conduct belies their lack of material wealth. Margaret, though, is not intimidated by her poverty and continues to behave as though she is the daughter of a curate.

While they are a solace to the dying Bessy, the most important purpose of Margaret's visits for us as readers is to introduce us to the factory workers who underpin Milton-Northern's prosperity. Bessy's broken body is a reminder of the dangers involved in working in a factory, and her presence within the novel signals Gaskell's participation in a broader debate about factory conditions and legislation, such as the Factory Acts of 1850 and 1856, which sought to regulate working hours for women and children. The novel appeared in weekly parts in Dickens' journal, *Household Words*, which regularly ran articles on factories, strikes and industrial accidents. These articles would have added to the reader's understanding of the novel's social context, explaining conflicts between masters and workers and offering readers a sense of factory life.

North and South was preceded in the journal by Dickens' own attempt at writing an industrial novel, *Hard Times,* and since the journal's circulation doubled during this period, it is safe to say that readers were developing an appetite for industrial fiction and stories about the North of England. Gaskell, who had difficulty adhering to the rigid constraints of writing in serial format, seems to have been concerned that Dickens would impinge on her territory, to the extent that he had to reassure her that there would be no strikes in his novel. However, Gaskell's writing is in many ways much more authentic in its depiction of the North than Dickens', not least because she lived among the people she depicts in her novels and understood the difficult conditions in which factory hands lived.

Bessy Higgins is Gaskell's attempt to draw her readers into the discussion about the need to regulate factories. Sent out to work at an early age, by the time Margaret meets her, Bessy is dying because her lungs are congested with cotton fluff. Anxious to capture and respect the working-class voice and the Manchester dialect, Gaskell allows Bessy to tell the story in her own words:

> Some folk have a great wheel at one end o' their carding-rooms to make a draught, and carry off th' dust; but that wheel costs a deal o' money – five or six hundred pound, maybe, and brings in no profit; so it's but a few of th' masters as will put 'em up; and I've heard tell o' men who didn't like working in places where there was a wheel, because they said as how it made 'em hungry, at after they'd been long used to swallowing fluff, tone go without it, and that their wage ought to be raised if they were to work in such places. So between masters and men th' wheels fall through. I know I wish there'd been a wheel in our place, though. (102)

What is particularly horrific about this scene is the knowledge that some workers are so ravenously hungry that the fluff they inhale has become a part of their diet, acting to suppress their appetites. Gaskell doesn't romanticize the workers and here exemplifies how they are, at times, complicit in their own undoing.

Gaskell takes care to allow the people to speak in their own voices. Her ear for Mancunian accents may not always catch the cadences of her characters' speech, yet Bessy's practical, matter-of-fact account evokes sympathy for the young woman, without over-sentimentalizing her plight. Bessy is a flawed human being, who is prone to melancholy and who clings to apocalyptic visions of the afterlife. Margaret certainly does not approve of her yearning for the afterlife, but Bessy's feelings highlight the utter misery of her present existence. Unable to find physical or psychological comfort in the present, death is the only solace available to Bessy.

Gaskell uses *North and South* as a way of highlighting the divisions between masters and workers, but in the end she wishes to stress a shared humanity and attempts to show how there might be unity between the two groups. As a clear-sighted outsider, Margaret is able to point out the dependency between the factory owners and the 'hands' who work for them, expressing her deep surprise at the lack of connectedness between the two factions:

> I see two classes dependent on each other in every possible way, yet each evidently regarding the interests of the other as opposed

> to their own; I never lived in a place before where there were two sets of people always running each other down. (118)

Ultimately, it is Margaret the displaced outsider who manages to bring the two groups together. She teaches Mr Thornton the doctrine of *noblesse oblige*, that position comes with responsibility, and as the novel closes we see the pair on the brink of forming not just a matrimonial alliance, but also a partnership of values, which will combine Thornton's Northern practicality with Margaret's compassion and understanding. In defaulting to the marriage plot, this closure does not tackle the broader issues of industrialism and poverty that Gaskell has exposed in the novel. However, it does place the onus on the middle-class couple (and by implication the middle-class reader) to assist the workers from their position of wealth and power.

Jane Eyre and genteel poverty

While both Dickens and Gaskell engage with some of the most impoverished members of society, *Jane Eyre* examines what happens when those born into more fortunate families fell upon hard times. Jane occupies an anomalous class position in that she exemplifies what the Victorians termed 'genteel poverty'. Although well educated, Jane is required to earn her own living and represents a growing group of women who lacked resources of their own and who could not depend upon the support of family members. Like *Oliver Twist*, *Jane Eyre* is an orphan narrative, although Jane spends much of the novel attempting to resist the dependent status of the parentless child.

It is important to Jane that she is able to earn her own living and indeed she is slightly contemptuous of women, like Blanche Ingram, who have nothing to do but attract a wealthy husband. Jane is ferocious in asserting her independence, expressing discomfort at the 'unnatural and strange' (227) jewels that Rochester wishes to bestow upon her after their engagement and resisting his desire to dress her in rich fabrics. In the awkward pre-wedding shopping excursion in chapter 24, Rochester draws on what we would now term (after Edward Said) 'Orientalist' imagery to figure himself as a polygamous grand Turk, a parallel that becomes increasingly uncomfortable after his attempt at bigamous marriage is exposed. Jane is deeply troubled by what she calls the 'Eastern allusion', comparing Rochester to a slave owner and suggesting that he is frivolous with his 'spare cash' (237). She then goes on to think about herself in relation to Rochester's former mistress, commenting:

> I only want an easy mind, sir; not crushed by crowded obligations. Do you remember what you said of Céline Varens? – of the diamonds, the cashmeres you gave her? I will not be your English Céline Varens. I shall continue to act as Adèle's governess; by that I shall earn my board and lodging, and thirty pounds a year besides. I'll furnish my own wardrobe out of that money, and you shall give me nothing but . . . [y]our regard: and if I give you mine in return, that debt will be quit. (237, my ellipses)

Jane here shows that she is eager not to become a 'kept' woman even within her marriage, believing that Rochester's respect for her will diminish if she allows him to shower her with possessions. Having previously been dependent upon her Aunt Reed who, along with Jane's cousins, constantly reminded her of her inferior, dependent status, it is hardly surprising that Jane's self-esteem is bound up with her ability to keep herself.

Jane demonstrates a similar pride when she flees Thornfield Hall and its temptations, leaving behind the jewels purchased for the 'visionary bride' (281) and taking only the 20 shillings that belong to her, the clothing she has bought for herself and a few small personal possessions. Shortly afterwards, when the emotionally exhausted Jane finds herself totally destitute, having given all of her money to a coach driver to take her as far away from Rochester as he can, she is left hungry and distraught, to sleep in the open. Unaccustomed to begging, Jane's genteel pride gets the better of her when she finds herself unable to barter a handkerchief or her gloves in exchange for a cake of bread. She declares, 'I was seized with shame: my tongue would not utter the request I had prepared' (287) and although her plain, respectable appearance disguises her penury, the fact that she does not make a purchase means that she is unable to linger in the bakery.

In attempting to find employment that matches her refined yet impoverished position, Jane tries to find work as a dressmaker, then a servant and then, out of desperation, asks whether women are employed in a nearby needle factory. The response she receives to one of her questions, 'Poor folk mun get on as they can' (287), reveals society's lack of provision for women in Jane's circumstances. Her neat attire makes her an object of suspicion as she knocks on people's doors and not even the clergyman's housekeeper is willing to help her. Jane registers the incongruity of her situation when she reports that a farmer who gives her a slice of bread believes her to be 'an eccentric sort of lady who has taken a fancy to his brown loaf' (289–90). However, the fact that she is later forced to beg for cold porridge destined to feed a pig should alert us to the true horror of her situation. Sleeping rough and wandering aimlessly, Jane exposes herself to danger, and it is probable that only her respectable clothing saves her from arrest under the Vagrancy Act.

In a slightly implausible plot twist, Brontë eventually removes her heroine from peril by allowing her to be taken in by the Rivers family, who fortuitously turn out to be her cousins. In spite of her reduced circumstances, Jane equivocates when Hannah, the housekeeper who had previously turned her away, declares her to be a 'beggar'. Jane berates Hannah, declaring,

> But I do think hardly of you . . . and I'll tell you why – not so much because you refused to give me shelter, or regarded me as an impostor, as because you just now made it a species of reproach that I had no 'brass' and no house. Some of the best people that ever lived have been as destitute as I am; and if you are a Christian, you ought not to consider poverty a crime. (301)

In spite of her protestations, Jane *is* a beggar at this point in the novel. She clings to her accomplishments as though they will somehow save her from the stigma of penury, but the fact is that she has nothing to call her own and is utterly dependent upon the charity of the Rivers family. Jane's pride and independence are admirable in Victorian terms, as is her desire to work. However, her situation points to the extreme vulnerability of the unprotected female and all too many women in Jane's position would have slipped into prostitution of one form or another in order to stay alive.

Eliot, Hardy and rural poverty

The Victorians focused a great deal of their attention on urban poverty as a by-product of industrialism. Although it may not have been such a visible concern, rural penury was also a significant issue and a number of Victorian novels engage with the encroachment of the town onto the countryside. This concern is evident in *Oliver Twist* when Bill Sikes moves from the centre of London to Chertsey, where he plans to commit a robbery, and is presented as a type of contaminant, bringing metropolitan evil into the countryside. Many Victorian novels show the expansion of cities, which gradually swallow up rural areas and those who live there and both George Eliot and Thomas Hardy shared an interest in how urbanism was reshaping the rural.

According to Raymond Williams in *The Country and the City*, if we read Thomas Hardy's novels as mere tales of Wessex, we miss one of their central points, which is the ways in which life in the countryside was changing so that distant market forces began to have a colossal influence on local economies and communities (Williams, 1973: 209). Williams argues that in *The Mayor of Casterbridge* Henchard is the architect of his own downfall because, like Maggie Tulliver's father in *The Mill on the Floss*, he is unable to adapt to these economic shifts:

> Henchard is not destroyed by a new and alien kind of dealing but by a development of his own trade which he has himself invited. It is Henchard in Casterbridge who speculates in grain as he had speculated in people; he is in every sense, within an observed way of life, a dealer and a destructive one; his strength compromised by that. (209)

Henchard is a successful speculator so long as he maintains a virtual monopoly on grain in Casterbridge. When Susan Henchard arrives in Casterbridge to find the husband who sold her, the people are complaining at having been sold 'growed wheat' (32). Solomon Longways goes on to explain Henchard's power and wealth, commenting, 'Never a big dealing in wheat, barley, oats, hay, roots, and such-like but Henchard's got a hand in it. Ay, and he'll go into other things, too; and that's where he makes his mistake' (37).

Although Solomon is here speaking of Henchard's power and wealth, he also highlights the weakness of the Mayor's strategy in spreading his investments across a range of goods. It becomes clear when Farfrae arrives that the Mayor's knowledge of corn is basic and out of touch with scientific and technological developments. Alarmingly, though, while Henchard is able to dismiss the inedible grain as one of 'the accidents of a large business' (38), he fails to take into account the centrality of bread to the working man's diet. The sale of the bad wheat has particularly unpleasant consequences for the poorest men and women in Casterbridge, who are left in extreme discomfort from consuming it.

While the plots of both *The Mill on the Floss* and *The Mayor of Casterbridge* revolve around characters in reasonably privileged positions who experience social descent, both texts also include minor characters who represent the world of rural poverty. When Maggie decides that she will be queen of the gypsies (book I, chapter 11), for instance, she is slightly aghast to discover that the travellers cannot provide her with bread, butter or treacle and while the narrator points this out humorously as a deficiency in her education, the incident points to a lack of class awareness on the little girl's part. Maggie's view of the gypsies is romanticized and she is horrified to be served a foul-smelling stew that is clearly made from scraps and poached meat. Although the narrator does not dwell on the incident, the gypsies represent both an itinerant society under threat and some of the challenges associated with penury in the countryside. Similarly, in *The Mayor of Casterbridge* although they are not prominent, characters like the old furmity seller and Abel Whittle are reminders of the extreme poverty in the countryside. Indeed, although Mrs Goodenough, the furmity woman, is reasonably prosperous when she appears in the opening chapters, when she returns to appear before Henchard in court 20 years later her appearance reflects a life of poverty and alcohol abuse, suggesting that her product is no longer in demand. At the same time, Whittle (whom I shall discuss in more detail in the section on 'Masculinity') has few options open to him, other than working for Henchard.

Unlike an industrial 'hand' who might move from factory to factory in prosperous times, Whittle and his neighbours must either toil for the ill-tempered mayor, or leave their community behind. This dilemma is exemplified by the incident in chapter 13, when Hardy shows us a farmer and his son, forced to take work some distance away. Although the son's sweetheart, Nelly, seems somewhat melodramatic when she declares 'Thirty-five mile! . . . I shall never see 'ee again!' (162, my ellipses), she points to a prohibitive distance in a world where transportation was restricted to horseback, cart or foot. The young man's comment 'I can't starve father' (162) highlights the climate of agrarian depression in which the novel was set and emphasizes the vulnerability of those who worked on the land in an age where machinery was beginning to displace the farm hand. This pair is fortunate, in that Farfrae takes pity on them, but in other works, such as *Tess of the d'Urbervilles*, Hardy highlighted the role of machinery in driving workers from the land.

The city

The Northern manufacturing city

Most of the action in Gaskell's *North and South* takes place in Milton-Northern, a city with more than a passing resemblance to Manchester. By using her protagonist Margaret Hale to mediate her accounts of working-class life Gaskell is able to guide her readers through the complete otherness of the Northern industrial experience. This process is exemplified through the scene in which Margaret arrives in the city, fresh from a sheltered life in genteel London and rural Helstone:

> For several miles before they reached Milton, they saw a deep lead-coloured cloud hanging over the horizon in the direction in which it lay. It was all the darker from contrast with the pale gray-blue of the wintry sky . . . Nearer to the town, the air had a faint taste and smell of smoke; perhaps, after all, more a loss of the fragrance of grass and herbage than any positive taste or smell. Quick they were whirled over long, straight, hopeless streets of regularly-built houses, all small and of brick. Here and there a great oblong many-windowed factory stood up, like a hen among her chickens, puffing out black 'unparliamentary' smoke, and sufficiently accounting for the cloud which Margaret

> had taken to foretell rain. As they drove through the larger and wider streets, from the station to the hotel, they had to stop constantly; great loaded lurries blocked up the not over-wide thoroughfares. Margaret had now and then been into the city in her drives with her aunt. But there the heavy lumbering vehicles seemed various in their purposes and intent; here every van, every waggon and truck, bore cotton, either in the raw shape in bags, or the woven shape in bales of calico. People thronged the footpaths, most of them well-dressed as regarded the material, but with a slovenly looseness which struck Margaret as different from the shabby, threadbare smartness of a similar class in London. (59)

Here, Gaskell skilfully introduces the reader to the noise and pollution of the manufacturing city, as well as its dizzying energy. Milton-Northern could not be more different from the rambling rose-covered parsonage Margaret has left behind her, and Gaskell effectively captures the shock of the new by undercutting her character's expectations. Believing that her brief excursions with her aunt have prepared her for her new life, Margaret is overwhelmed by the bustle and the omnipresence of the trade on which the North's prosperity is founded. So dominant is the cotton industry, that it repeatedly disrupts her journey across the city, as the traffic gives way to the transported calico. The political theorist Friedrich Engels remarked in 1844 that Manchester was a rigidly segregated community, 'The town itself is peculiarly built, so that a person may live in it for years, and go in and out daily without coming into contact with a working-people's quarter or even with workers'. He continues to note that those belonging to what he terms the 'money aristocracy', 'can take the shortest road through the middle of all the labouring districts to their places of business, without ever seeing that they are in the midst of the grimy misery that lurks to the right and the left' (Engels, 2001: 49). Thus, Margaret's observations of Milton-Northern life in this scene and in the many later passages where she walks though the slums also offer a subtle reminder of her own class descent; this is a world that would normally be unknown to the well-bred young woman.

Gaskell depicts the metropolitan experience as an affront to Margaret's refined, Southern sensibilities, as she inhales the all-pervasive factory smoke and compares the urban dwellers to the more sophisticated, stylish Londoners. While highlighting the sheer difference of life in the industrial heartland, the narrator also takes the opportunity to draw attention to Margaret's Southern prejudices and snobbery, using judgemental terms like 'slovenly' and 'shabby' to convey the contrast between London and Milton. In this regard, Gaskell was tapping into the type of civic pride responsible for the magnificent, imposing town halls that the Victorians built in Northern manufacturing cities like Bradford, Leeds and Manchester. These structures, which are still standing today, were a way for the emerging manufacturing powers to signal their rivalry with and financial supremacy over London.

London

If the mid-Victorian city seemed sprawling and overwhelming, by the end of the century the metropolis was rapidly expanding and urban culture was becoming increasingly central to the British way of life. Although the city was for many a source of excitement and energy, it was also a site of danger and vice. Dickens had figured London as a labyrinth in *Bleak House* and this Gothic vision of an unknowable, maze-like city became increasingly poignant as the nineteenth century came to a close. Crime writers including Sir Arthur Conan Doyle explored the imaginative possibilities of a bewilderingly large city that could never be fully policed or controlled, and one of the most famous literary images of the end of the century has to be that of Doyle's Professor Moriarty lurking like a spider at the centre of a web of urban crime.

In *Oliver Twist*, Dickens sets up a clear contrast between the country and the city, introducing his readers to some of the most notorious areas of London. So shocking was his depiction of the criminal slum area, or 'rookery', Jacob's Island, that Dickens was forced to defend its existence in a preface to the novel when Alderman Peter Laurie (a magistrate and former Lord Mayor of London) claimed that there was no such place. It is clear from Dickens' depictions of London that he sees the city as a source of contamination. At the beginning of chapter XXI, when Oliver is dragged away from Fagin's lair and forced to participate in a robbery, the narrator emphasizes the city's infernal qualities. Oliver is bewildered by the 'roar of sound and bustle' (152) and the 'tumult of discordant sounds' (153), while Dickens draws attention to the pestilence at the heart of the city by describing not only the dirt and grime that accompanies metropolitan living, but also the overpowering smells:

> It was market-morning. The ground was covered, nearly ankle-deep, with filth and mire; a thick steam, perpetually rising from the reeking bodies of the cattle, and mingling with the fog, which seemed to rest upon the chimney-tops, hung heavily above. All the pens in the centre of the large area, and as many temporary pens as could be crowded into the vacant space, were filled with sheep; tied up to posts by the gutter side were long lines of beasts and oxen, three or four deep. Countrymen, butchers, drovers, hawkers, boys, thieves, idlers, and vagabonds of every low grade, were mingled together in a mass; the whistling of drovers, the barking dogs, the bellowing and plunging of the oxen, the bleating of sheep, the grunting and squeaking of pigs, the cries of hawkers, the shouts, oaths, and quarrelling on all sides; the ringing of bells and roar of voices, that issued from every public-house; the crowding, pushing, driving, beating, whooping and yelling; the hideous and discordant dim that resounded from every corner of the market; and the unwashed, unshaven, squalid, and dirty figures constantly running to and fro, and bursting in and out of the throng; rendered it a stunning and bewildering scene, which quite confounded the senses. (153)

This passage captures the sensory experience of city life in the early nineteenth century, but at the same time its 'filth and mire' point to more widespread pestilence that goes beyond the smell of animal excrement. The idlers and vagabonds lingering on the streets suggest that the villainy of Fagin's gang is an endemic part of life in London and perhaps a by-product of the crowding and struggling that Dickens describes. Focusing on city's soundscape, in addition to its sights and smells, this extract effectively conveys Oliver's terror and awe when confronted with the seedier side of the capital.

As the chapter continues and Oliver travels further from London to the scene of the intended crime, Sikes is figured as a type of pollutant, spreading from the city into the countryside.

While the passage above describes a fog that partly reflects the smoky atmosphere of the nineteenth-century city, it also suggests a type of moral fog, obscuring connections between people. Thus, while Sikes leaves the city, he is accompanied by an eerie mist, which transforms into a 'heavy fog' (161) in the next chapter as Sikes, Crackit and Barney make their way to Chertsey, with Oliver in tow. Travelling with the criminals, this fog seems to be a miasmatic representation of their evil, moving through the air to invade the pastoral idyll. Dickens identifies the criminal gang so closely with the city, that even after Sikes has murdered Nancy, he still gravitates back (see chapter 50), although escape to the countryside would be a wiser policy.

In spite of, or perhaps because of, its dangers, the city remained a source of great attraction with its diverse population and huge crowds. Apparently respectable men would live in one part of London with their wives and families, while keeping a mistress elsewhere in the city or the suburbs. Although he is associated with Transylvania in our imaginations, Stoker's *Dracula* spends most of the novel in London. The vampire is drawn to the anonymity of London and signals his affinity for city life by renaming himself 'Count de Ville' (literally meaning 'of the town'). Strategically placing coffins of earth across the city, Dracula accumulates metropolitan properties in order to conceal himself. In a moment of entirely characteristic panic, Jonathan Harker looks down at the sleeping, sated Count and understands why he is drawn to the English capital. Harker tells us, 'This was the being I was helping to transfer to London, where, perhaps, for centuries to come he might, amongst its teeming millions, satiate his lust for blood, and create a new and ever-widening circle of semi-demons to batten on the helpless' (51). In Transylvania Dracula is feared, to the extent that the peasants cross themselves when they learn where Jonathan is going. In London, however, almost everyone is oblivious to the Count's presence and Stoker thus expands the traditional Gothic form, whereby a character is pursued through a labyrinthine castle or stately home to create a new imperial Gothic. The maze-like city of London thus becomes the site of a much larger scale of pursuit in which the stakes have risen from the plight of an individual hero or heroine to the whole of society. Thus, as the metropolis expanded, so too did its narrative and imaginative possibilities.

Education

George Eliot was deeply aware of the limitations of women's education, and the issue was one that was important to her personally. In her essay 'Silly Novels by Lady Novelists' (1856) she attacked the frivolity of some of the literary works aimed at women, suggesting that they were complicit in reinforcing the gender divide by providing vacuous female characters for impressionable women to imitate. She commented:

> And the most mischievous form of feminine silliness is the literary form, because it tends to confirm the popular prejudice against the more solid education of women. When men see girls wasting their time in consultations about bonnets and ball dresses, and in giggling or sentimental love-confidences, or middle-aged women mismanaging their children, and solacing themselves with acrid gossip, they can hardly help saying, 'For Heaven's sake, let girls be better educated; let them have some better objects of thought – some more solid occupations'. (2009: 135)

Eliot used her fiction to highlight the shortcomings of women's learning and to emphasize that a well-educated woman would make a much more helpful partner in life. In *Middlemarch* (1874), for instance, the character Rosamond Vincy attends a finishing school in which she is taught the graceful art of stepping into and out of a carriage, but she learns nothing that will prepare her to be the wife of a provincial doctor. Dinah Birch has commented that, 'A defective education blights the lives of many of George Eliot's fictional girls' (2008: 112). However, far from believing that everyone should be exposed to the same educational opportunities, Eliot wished to see an abolition of the hierarchy of knowledge, which saw some forms of learning valued above others. As she noted in a letter, 'the deepest disgrace is to do work for which we are unfit – to do any sort of work badly' (quoted in Flint, 2001: 165).

In some ways a textual figure for Eliot herself, Maggie Tulliver would clearly have benefited more from the education that her brother receives, on the strength of his gender, rather than his abilities. Maggie is able to master Tom's assignments swiftly, while her brother's mind moves 'with a slow, half-stifled pulse in a medium of uninteresting or unintelligible ideas' (264). The narrative voice offers a biting critique of the education offered to Tom, noting that since Mr Tulliver is unable to understand everything his son learns he does not complain, even though he laments the absence of maps and 'summing' (264). Furthermore, Tom's schooling is shown to be a consequence of his father's pretensions to social mobility, rather than the type of knowledge that will aid him in life. This point is brought home somewhat brutally after Mr Tulliver is bankrupted, when Tom's Uncle Deane tells him,

> Your poor father went the wrong way in giving you an education . . . you've had a sort of learning that's all very well for a young fellow like our Mr. Stephen Guest, who'll have nothing to do but sign cheques all his life, and may as well have Latin inside his head as any other sort of stuffing. (314)

Tom's education is impractical and instead of preparing him for the challenges ahead, it diminishes his confidence. Tom himself points to the absurdity of his lessons when he talks to Philip Wakem about the 'education of a gentleman' in chapter 3 of book two (236). While Tom is excited by the violence and heroics of the ancient Greeks, he sees no reason to apply himself to classical study.

Maggie, on the other hand, is thoughtful, quick and able, although the fact that she has to direct her own learning leaves her vulnerable when she encounters the teachings of Thomas à Kempis and internalizes them. Unable to approach à Kempis critically or objectively, Maggie turns herself into a living martyr and almost marries Philip Wakem out of a sense of duty. Part of Maggie's attraction to her cousin's fiancé, Stephen Guest, extends from her admiration of his learning as is demonstrated when she becomes absorbed in his account of the Bridgewater Treatises, which attempted to reconcile geological discoveries with the biblical account of the Creation. Maggie's hunger to learn sees her unselfconsciously leaning forward like a 'downy-lipped alumnus' listening to a professor (489), but it does not protect her from Guest's predatory male gaze. Stephen thus exploits and manipulates Maggie's desire to learn, eventually compromising her reputation by almost persuading her to abscond with him. In comparison with her more conventionally accomplished cousin Lucy, Maggie is an astonishingly original and well-read young woman, and this is one of the reasons she becomes so appealing to Guest.

Like Maggie Tulliver, Elizabeth-Jane in *The Mayor of Casterbridge* is an autodidact, educating herself through an eclectic range of reading that would not always be considered suitable for a young woman. She is highly conscious of the deficiencies in her education and understands when she is adopted by Henchard that though she has fine clothes, they cannot disguise her lack of cultivation.

> There is something wrong in all this . . . If they only knew what an unfinished girl I am – that I can't talk Italian, or use globes, or show any of the accomplishments they learn at boarding schools – how they would despise me! Better sell all this finery and buy myself grammar-books, and dictionaries, and a history of all the philosophies. (97)

Later, at the beginning of chapter 20, Henchard berates her for her use of dialect as well as her unladylike handwriting, which curiously seems to align her with the late-Victorian New Woman, 'It was a splendid round bold hand of her own conception, a style that would have stamped a woman as Minerva's own in more recent days' (131). While Elizabeth-Jane's writing may signify her originality, Henchard's reaction reveals the ways in which education often became tangled up with questions of status. Henchard worries that his stepdaughter's hand does not befit her position as the mayor's daughter, just as Mr Tulliver needs Tom to receive a classical education to reflect his social pretensions. Mr Thornton in *North and South* shows a similar proclivity, although in his case his desire to be educated is bound up with a moral curiosity and development that make his lessons with Mr Hale significantly more than rote-learning.

The issue of education is an important one for Charlotte Brontë too, although her concern is less tied to gender than that of Eliot or Hardy. Having been a governess herself, Brontë is critical of unregulated schools in *Jane Eyre*, where she engages with a number of important educational issues. When Jane is sent away to school by her aunt, Mrs Reed, the haven she anticipates turns out to be a place of terror, where girls are bullied into compliance. Lowood Institution is a charity school for orphans that is funded through subscriptions paid by those living in the vicinity, and in this respect it is similar to the workhouse in *Oliver Twist*, where, in spite of his amazing ability to read, we never actually see Oliver learn anything. Lowood is directed and administered by the son of the founder and it is almost completely unregulated. As a consequence, the girls live in fear of the regular humiliations meted out to them when they fail to measure up to the standards of learning and behaviour demanded by the director, Mr Brocklehurst.

Brontë clearly identifies the tyranny within the school with the male authority of Mr Brocklehurst, who appears almost phallic when Jane looks up to see him as a 'long black column . . . looking longer, narrower, and more rigid than ever' (53). Brocklehurst demonstrates an almost sadistic cruelty when having ordered one child's unruly curls to be shorn from her head, he then declares that all of the girls must have their top knots removed. Hair in nineteenth-century fiction is often associated with sexuality and Brocklehurst's actions suggest that he fears the untamed female. When Brocklehurst justifies his decision, he does so not by invoking the need for hygiene in an environment where girls live in close proximity and where disease or parasites can spread rapidly, but by asserting that he must 'mortify in these girls the lusts of the flesh' (56), using the language of a despot, rather than a teacher.

Lowood becomes a more reasonable place when Brocklehurst is removed, and Jane receives a sufficiently broad education to be able to work as a governess. However, Brontë's concern with educational matters does not dissipate, since Jane goes on to teach Rochester's illegitimate daughter, who is more concerned with gifts and clothes than she is with learning. Once again, Brontë highlights the abuse of education when Blanche Ingram asks Rochester why he did not simply send his ward to school, before continuing to detail the many tricks she and her sisters played upon their long-suffering governess (155). Rochester echoes her view of the school as a type of dumping ground for unwanted children when, following his engagement to Jane, he threatens repeatedly to send Adèle away.

While Adèle's education seems like a lost cause because she has inherited her French mother's frivolity, Jane shows when she runs the village school at Morton that she is committed to a much more benevolent form of instruction than she herself experienced. At the beginning of chapter 31 she details the shortcomings of her new students, pointing to the challenges involved in educating working children:

> But three of the number can read: none write or cipher. Several knit, and a few sew a little. They speak with the broadest accent of the district. At present, they and I have a difficulty in understanding each other's language. Some of them are unmannered, rough, intractable, as well as ignorant; but others are docile, have a wish to learn, and evince a disposition that pleases me. (315)

While Jane struggles to begin with, not least with her preconceptions about the abilities and potential of her pupils, her perseverance is rewarded and she comments, 'I found some of these heavy-looking, gaping rustics wake up into sharp-witted girls enough' (322). While her initial – and somewhat offensive – assessment is tinged by class prejudice, her discovery that the girls are worth teaching is an important one in the context of contemporary discussions about working-class education, as well as the schooling of young girls.

By the end of the nineteenth century the debate about women's access to education had taken centre stage, with the New Woman demanding the same access to schools and universities as her brothers. One of the underlying reasons was that the growing number of women who had no prospect of marriage and no family resources to draw upon found that their educations did not adequately prepare them for life in the wider world. We might contrast the figures of Lucy Westenra and Mina Harker from *Dracula* to gain a clearer sense of the skills needed by the less affluent woman. Attractive and wealthy, Lucy receives no fewer than three proposals and it is clear that she will never need to work for her living. Mina, on the other hand, must make the most of her education and is constantly looking for new skills. Although she wishes to support her husband, the fact that Mina learns shorthand and typing aligns her with the late-Victorian 'typewriter girl' who flouted convention by earning her keep and living independently and signals her potential for radical or shocking behaviour.

In a world where young women were demanding the right to take degrees, Mina's actions are comparatively modest. The end of the century saw the emergence of the 'Girton Girl', an affluent type of young woman who attended classes at Cambridge and who was parodied by a number of novelists including Grant Allen in *The Woman Who Did*, whereas Mina simply wishes to take advantage of modern inventions to be able to assist Jonathan in his work. Nevertheless, when Mina begins to use her uncanny ability to remember railway timetables and other skills to pursue the Count, Van Helsing tells her that she has a 'man's brain' (234). The fact that the vampire is drawn to her suggests that she has overstepped the boundaries of propriety, however, and as Sally Ledger commented, Stoker 'wanted to terminate the career of the sexualized New Woman and to reinstate in her place a modernized version of the "angel in the house"' (Ledger, 1997: 106). In Stoker's world the education of women was a pragmatic step, rather than a progressive one, and it would take many more years before society could accept the education of women as a basic right.

Darwin

The Mill on the Floss

As I discussed in Part One, the publication of Charles Darwin's *On the Origin of Species* in 1859 created shockwaves throughout the Victorian intelligentsia as they tried to reconcile Darwin's explanation of evolution with religious teachings. George Eliot, as an atheist, did not face these challenges and was fascinated by the imaginative possibilities that Darwin's theory presented, although as Angelique Richardson notes, the novel *The Mill on the Floss* is a more general reflection on the nineteenth-century interest in heredity (2003: 85). Published a year after Darwin's controversial book (although she had already written volume one before *The Origin* appeared), Eliot's novel is brimming with references to what was later termed 'natural selection' and contains a number of fascinating references to breeding and hybridity.

When Maggie is first introduced to us, the narrator tells us that she is a 'small mistake of nature' (61), suggesting that she is some type of anomaly. While most of the characters are unsophisticated, they nevertheless discuss breeding and behavioural characteristics, attempting to understand why Maggie is both intelligent but unable to conform, while her brother Tom is given to action, rather than thought. Maggie's father knows that his daughter is like him and blames his wife for his son's weakness of intellect. He reflects:

> It seems a bit of a pity, though . . . as the lad should take after the mother's side instead o' the little wench. That's the worst on't wi' the crossing o' breeds: you can never justly calkilate what'll come on't. (59)

This discussion of breeding and fitness pervades the novel and the narrator extends the metaphor to consider both the natural and the economic worlds. While Maggie's cleverness marks her out as a forerunner of the New Woman, who emerged at the end of the nineteenth century, her context means that she cannot be neatly assimilated into her parochial, closed-minded society. Eliot's novel reflects the period of her own childhood when a lively, impulsive young woman like Maggie (or Eliot) would have presented a challenge to her parents and to the world around her.

Maggie is one of a sequence of Eliot's heroines who possess remarkable potential, but who are thwarted by social pressures. Although she is fiercely clever, she is also curiously naïve about the world, believing that when she runs away to join the gypsies she will immediately become their queen and failing to think through the consequences of her intrigue with Stephen Guest. In this respect, she fails to adapt to the changing world around her and seems unable to pick up a number of basic social rules, demonstrating that she is unable to modify herself according to her environment. She is, perhaps, like Arthur Henry Hallam in Tennyson's *In Memoriam*, a 'herald of a higher race' (118.14), born before society can accommodate her and her difference.

The novel contains a number of proleptic moments (i.e. moments in which events prefigure the conclusion) and several of these draw implicit comparisons between Tom and Maggie and hybrid creatures of the natural world. When Maggie discovers that she has killed Tom's lop-eared rabbits though neglect, Luke consoles her by pointing to their lack of vigour and observing, 'Things out o' nature niver thrive. God A'mighty doesn't like 'em. He made the rabbits' ears to lie back, an it's nothing but contrariness to make 'em hing down like a mastiff dog's' (82). A similar critique follows a few pages later when Tom Tulliver's dog, Yap is shown to be a spoiled companion animal who is inadequate when measured against the working dogs admired by Bob Jakin. When Yap tries to bite Bob, he is simply flung into the river, where his soaking anticipates Tom and Maggie's final immersion in the Floss. Bob, on the other hand, later compares himself to his own dog, Mumps, who is a mongrel and who is therefore more robust and less highly strung, emphasizing that Bob is well adapted for the world he inhabits. Mary Jean Corbett takes this argument a step forward, suggesting that the mongrel was for Eliot and her contemporaries, 'a figure for the English themselves as a people of hybrid stock' (Corbett, 2007: 132) and this reading sits neatly alongside arguments that suggest that the English middle classes were drawn to the theory of evolution because it validated their own rise to economic dominance.

If there is any character in Eliot's world who is able to adapt and survive, then it is Bob. When he is first introduced to us, he is presented as a slightly wild, uncouth character who frightens Maggie, but who, significantly, knows all about the natural world where class and birth are meaningless. Feeling a misplaced confidence in his place in the social hierarchy, Tom patronizes Bob as 'an inferior who could always be treated with authority in spite of his superior knowingness' (101). Bob rejects Tom's assertion of mastery over him, understanding that birthright is no longer a guarantee of one's place within the social hierarchy and that with hard work social mobility is possible. Unlike Tom, Bob is entrepreneurial and becomes a type of small-scale capitalist or speculator, combining his business acumen with compassion when he invites Tom to lay out some money in order to gain interest. Although Tom makes money, it is not because of his abilities, but because of Bob's willingness to assist him and because of his natural skill as a salesman.

In economic terms Maggie's father is also unable to adapt to changes in the wider world. Mr Tulliver's business is conducted somewhat haphazardly, and although he wants his son to advance in life, he goes about it in the wrong way, attempting to turn Tom into something he is not, while neglecting Maggie's greater abilities. Eliot uses the language of miscegenation to consider Mr Tulliver's unfortunate match with his wife. Tulliver himself registers his culpability when he explains that he chose his wife 'cause she was a bit weak, like' (68) and because he did not wish to be argued with in his own home. He goes on to observe, 'when a man's got brains himself, there's no knowing where they'll run to; an' a pleasant sort o' soft woman may go on breeding you stupid lads and 'cute wenches, till it's like as if the world was turned topsy-turvy' (68–9). Tulliver has made a mistake in choosing a mate, which casts doubt on his own assertion of having 'brains'. The narrator shares this interpretation of Tom and Maggie as genetic accidents, remarking in the wake of Tulliver's illness that, 'mingled seed must bear a mingled crop' (462). This assessment, while ostensibly considering a day of mixed fortune, also resonates with the novel's interest in mixing and crossing breeds. Furthermore, the narrative voice casts doubt on Tulliver's own opinion of himself, noting his lack of vitality and inability to change in the wake of financial challenges:

> There are certain animals to which tenacity of position is a law of life – they can never flourish again after a single wrench: and there are certain human beings to whom predominance is a law of life and who can only sustain humiliation so long as they can refuse to believe in it, and, in their own conception, predominate still. (275)

Eliot's use of evolutionary language is innovative but not unique, and it is important to register that although he was certainly not as well versed in the latest scientific thinking as Eliot, Dickens had begun to think about class in biological terms in *Oliver Twist*. Thus Oliver's middle-class heritage is obvious to anyone with an ear for educated speech, whereas the villainous Bill Sikes bears a countenance that marks him out as a degenerate.

The Mayor of Casterbridge

Often compared to Eliot because of their shared interest in rural communities, Hardy's writing shows a similar concern with genealogy and lineage. Hardy was familiar with Darwin's work and, as Gillian Beer has noted, he was particularly concerned with 'imperfect adaptation' (Beer, 1983: 232). Given that the plot of *The Mayor of Casterbridge* revolves at least partly around the question of Elizabeth-Jane's parentage, it is hardly surprising to find references to breeding and ancestry that are often inflected by Darwinian thought. When Henchard first meets Farfrae, for instance, he scrutinizes his physiognomy, looking for a family resemblance that cannot be present. He declares, 'Your forehead, Farfrae, is something like my poor brother's . . . and the nose, too, isn't unlike his' (49), while noting at the same time that he lacks scientific knowledge. Later, when he has learned that Newson is Elizabeth-Jane's father, he looks at the young woman in her sleep to view 'buried genealogical facts, ancestral curves, dead men's traits' (126), able to read her origins only when her features are at rest.

Hardy thus exposes Henchard as a poor reader of faces, looking for signs that are not there in people who cannot be connected to him. More broadly, Henchard is like Maggie Tulliver's father, unable to change or develop, and as a result his business begins to decline once the more adaptable, up-to-date Farfrae appears. Stuck in the past (the narrator aligns him with the extinct Romans at the beginning of chapter 11 when we see him waiting among the ancient ruins), Henchard is doomed to see his family line extinguished, partly because of his propensity to drink, partly because of his lack of business acumen and partly because the one child he produces dies. In Darwinian terms the asexual mayor is a weak specimen, and it is perhaps only because of the small, enclosed nature of the Casterbridge community that he manages to be successful for so long.

Dracula

In *Dracula,* Bram Stoker taps into the debates that ensued from Darwin's discoveries, presenting the Count as a degenerate throwback whose criminal mind is equivalent to a child's brain (302). Van Helsing attempts to categorize Dracula in the final stages of his attempt to trap the vampire, telling Mina, 'The Count is a criminal and of criminal type. Nordau and Lombroso would so classify him, and *qua* criminal he is of an imperfectly formed mind' (342). In interpreting Dracula in this way, Van Helsing downplays his great intelligence and cunning, choosing to interpret it as a symptom of his atavism, rather than a sign of his superiority. Interestingly, early on in the novel Dracula looks to his ancestors for evidence of their strength and tenacity, viewing himself as part of a great line of warriors and asserting the dominance of his blood line in the 'whirlpool of European races' (28). While Van Helsing views Dracula as a throwback, the Count sees himself as part of an ancient tradition and asserts his superiority to the British men, most melodramatically when he proclaims, 'Your girls that you all love are mine already' (306). The Count's words, along with Van Helsing's assessment that he has 'infected' (360) Mina invoke contemporary fears of miscegenation (mixing breeds) and show the degree to which Darwin's discoveries had mutated into a source of terror for the late Victorians.

The representation of women

In the early pages of *North and South*, the formidable Mrs Thornton warns her prosperous and handsome son, John, 'rich husbands are reckoned prizes' (77). Although Mrs Thornton is attempting to cast doubt on Margaret's character, her comment cuts directly to the heart of the debate on marriage in the nineteenth century. The realist novel engages directly with the insinuation that marriage was no more than a licensed form of prostitution, offering a critique of the condition of women, although focusing particularly on the middle-class heroine and the very few choices open to her in defining her life.

Ian Watt has argued that realist writing is, from the eighteenth century onwards, driven by the 'courtship plot', whereby the female Bildungsroman focused not only on a young woman's development as a character, but also on her movement towards marriage (see Watt, 1957). However, by the middle of the nineteenth century, a number of novelists were becoming less patient with this formula and sought to refashion it. Thus, while *Jane Eyre* ends with an apparently happy marriage, Charlotte Brontë subverts a number of readerly expectations through the course of the novel, firstly thwarting our desire for the marriage between the Byronic Rochester and Jane, then refusing to allow Jane to marry the more conventionally attractive St. John Rivers. George Eliot offers an even bolder critique in *The Mill on the Floss*, where having established that Maggie Tulliver is unsuited for marriage, she refuses to condemn her character to its bonds, preferring to drown her rather than forcing her to submit or compromise.

Oliver Twist has been interpreted more recently as a novel detailing the breakdown of the courtship narrative, with Dickens depicting a 'monstrous marriage' at the centre of the work, which contaminates a number of other characters through its sheer toxicity (see Hager, 2010: 55–6). While the narrative voice is at pains to emphasize the essential purity of Oliver's mother, the novel's plot revolves around the boy's illegitimacy and the question mark surrounding his identity. The fact that Oliver is born outside of wedlock is a result of his father Edwin's failed marriage to an older woman, and, as Hager notes, 'It is, in fact, the failure of marriage that brings Oliver into being, just as it is the failure of marriage that situates him in such a way as to set in motion the novel's plot' (59). This interpretation suggests that Dickens' agenda is perhaps more subversive than it might initially appear to be, in a novel which appears to valorize middle-class respectability. Instead of upholding the institution of marriage, Dickens exposes its abuse and dangers. Although Leeford is a boy of nineteen when he is instructed by his father to marry, by the time he meets Agnes, Oliver's mother, he is an adult and should be aware of his responsibilities in relation to an innocent, vulnerable young woman. Nevertheless, the narrator distorts the usual cycle of blame and responsibility, suggesting that Leeford's wife, with her propensity for 'continental frivolities' (397) should be held responsible for the stain on Oliver's birth.

Women, prostitution and reputation

Although many Victorian novels revolved around characters from the middle classes, the figure of the prostitute haunted the genre. Then, as now, prostitution was a last resort for many women, although Victorian society largely viewed the 'fallen' women as responsible for their plight. The Victorians also had a much broader definition of what prostitution entailed. While today we would not regard women who have given birth outside of wedlock as prostitutes, for the Victorians there was more slippage between the categories of 'good' and 'bad' women. In Henry Mayhew's four-volume study, *London Labour and the London Poor* (1851–62), for instance, prostitutes are divided into six categories, including 'kept mistresses', 'sailors' and soldiers' women and thieves' women'. Mayhew went on to argue that 'she who confines her favours to one may still be a prostitute' before going on to suggest that prostitution was 'putting a woman's charms to vile uses' (36). Mayhew's assessment here downplays the socio-economic factors that often drove women to sell their bodies, suggesting that women are engaged in beguiling their clients, rather than forced into desperate acts.

Charles Dickens was sympathetic to the prostitute's plight, administering Urania Cottage, a 'home for fallen women', founded in 1847, on behalf of his friend, the philanthropist Angela Burdett Coutts. He also regularly represented prostitutes in his writing (for instance in *David Copperfield* and *Dombey and Son*) and, as Jenny Hartley has argued, 'the true victim of *Oliver Twist* is Nancy, and the villain is the street-life of London' (Hartley, 2008: 68). Elizabeth Gaskell shared Dickens' concern with the prostitute, and her novel *Ruth* (1853) is centred around a young woman who is seduced, then abandoned, while *Mary Barton* (1848) offers a sympathetic portrait of Mary's aunt, Esther, who works on the streets.

Dickens' decision to include a prostitute in *Oliver Twist* scandalized some of his early readers and he acknowledged in his preface to the third edition in 1841 that, 'it seems a very coarse and shocking circumstance that some of the characters in these pages are chosen from the most criminal and degraded of London's population . . . that the boys are pickpockets, and the girl is a prostitute' (liii). That Nancy is hardened and fallen when we first encounter her is without question. However, what is important about Dickens' representation is that in addition to gradually revealing Nancy's humane qualities through her care for the boys and her betrayal of Sikes in helping Oliver, we also learn the reasons behind her 'fall'. Moved by Oliver's innocence, Nancy turns on Fagin, berating him for her degraded state:

> I thieved for you when I was a child not half as old as this . . . I have been in the same trade, and in the same service for twelve years since . . . It is my living; and the cold, wet, dirty streets are my home; and you're the wretch that drove me to them long ago, and that'll keep me there, day and night, day and night till I die. (116, my ellipses)

Nancy's emotional outburst points to the vulnerability of young women in nineteenth-century London, revealing that she has been the victim of a predatory older man, who has driven her to a life of crime and debauchery. As the story unfolds, Nancy becomes a type of textual double for Oliver's 'fallen' mother, taking care of the boy and eventually forfeiting her life in order to protect him.

Women were, of course, not the only vulnerable people on the streets of London, and Larry Wolff has drawn attention to the dangers experienced by young boys, drawing on archival material from the 1830s to show the visibility of male prostitution at that time. While Dickens was writing his novel, the London Society for the Protection of Young Females and the Prevention of Prostitution was closing down brothels and prosecuting the people who ran them, many of whom were believed to be Jewish (Wolff, 1996: 236). Wolff goes on to establish a textual pairing of Fagin and Mr Brownlow, both of whom are referred to by Oliver as 'the old gentleman', noting that both are drawn to Oliver's good looks. Examining the scene in which Brownlow discusses Oliver with Mr Grimwig, Wolff reinterprets it as a 'comic connoisseurship of boys' (240) arguing that, 'Though Fagin appears as a force for the corruption, and Mr Brownlow for the redemption of the boy, the possibility of child prostitution in the novel threatens that clear distinction', continuing to suggest that the street-pacing Brownlow might be regarded in a more sinister light. Given that Oliver's innocent idealism is never overcome by his experiences, this interpretation of the extraordinarily benevolent Brownlow seems somewhat extreme. Nevertheless, Wolff is right to point out the many threats to which Oliver and the young pickpockets would have been exposed.

Reputation

In a world where young girls were raised to net the best possible husband, a woman's reputation was her most valuable asset and many Victorian novels explore the consequences of compromising a woman's good name. While in *Oliver Twist* Agnes is dead and cannot be harmed by slurs, the righteous Oliver is incensed when Noah Claypole declares 'She was a nice 'un, she was. Oh, Lor!' (41), while at the novel's opening the surgeon looks at Agnes' left hand, shakes his head and comments 'The old story! . . . no wedding ring, I see' (3). The surgeon's resigned air conveys the frequency with which he has seen women in this state, along with his society's intolerance for 'fallen' women. He does not explicitly cast judgement, but nor does he entertain the possibility that there may be an alternative explanation for Agnes' circumstances.

Nina Auerbach has compellingly argued that 'the Victorian imagination isolated the fallen woman pitilessly from a social context, preferring to imagine her as destitute and drowned prostitute or errant wife cast beyond the human community, because of her uneasy implication for wives who stayed at home' (1982: 159). At the root of her contention is the suggestion that the boundaries between the fallen woman and the wife were not at all clear, with marriage being tantamount to a legalized form of prostitution. As a consequence, those women who engaged in sexual activity outside of marriage were demonized and held responsible for a range of social evils, even though we would today regard them as a *symptom* of broader problems including poverty, rather than the cause. In spite of attempts to ostracize those who had 'fallen', many Victorians were well aware of the interchangeable nature of the wife and the prostitute.

Jane Eyre shows her awareness of the social and moral danger she is placed in by Mr Rochester's attempt to ensnare her in a bigamous marriage when she leaves the temptations of Thornfield Hall, fearing that she will yield to Mr Rochester if she remains. Having heard Rochester speak contemptuously of his former mistresses, she understands that if she succumbs to his entreaties she will not enjoy the safety afforded by marriage and runs the risk of being cast aside once her novelty value has diminished. Rochester himself admits that 'hiring a mistress is the next worst thing to buying a slave' (274) and Jane responds with caution to his attempts to reassure her of his loathing for the life he has left behind:

> I felt the truth of these words; and I drew from them the certain inference, that if I were so far to forget myself and all the teaching that had ever been instilled into me – under any pretext – with any justification – through any temptation – to become the successor of these poor girls, he would one day regard me with the same feeling which now in his mind desecrated their memory. (274)

Jane is ultimately rewarded for her strength of character when she is reunited with the recently widowed Rochester and able to become his wife. However, she had previously registered her knowledge of the high stakes at risk with the comment, 'That man had nearly made me his mistress: I must be ice and rock to him' (264). Jane is both too moral and too prudent to gamble with Rochester as his previous mistresses had done. She knows that without the legal contract of marriage to support her claim, she will be unprotected. Her later marriage to Rochester sees Jane in a much stronger position, since her maimed, blinded and emotionally wounded husband is far more dependent upon her than he would have been before. Feminist readers have suggested that this subdued version of Rochester is much more acceptable to the spirited Jane than the Byronic tyrant we encounter at the beginning of the novel, although Victorian readers would have been much more willing to subscribe to the idea of Rochester's redemption through a combination of suffering and the love of a good woman.

Those women who were not as cautious as Jane Eyre often faced a lifetime of social ostracism for their lapses in judgement. In *North and South,* Margaret Hale's good name is compromised, partly because of the ambiguity of her class status and partly because she does not behave with what was considered to be appropriate maidenly modesty. In the dramatic scene where Margaret defends Thornton against his protesting workers, she throws her arms around him to shield him from missiles thrown by the crowd. While this is one of several turning points in the tense relationship between Margaret and the man who will become her husband, it also points to the fragility of her reputation.

Thornton's formidable mother casts aspersions on Margaret's motives when she tells her son that he can 'hardly do otherwise' (188) than propose to her after what has passed. Although her intentions are pure, Margaret's actions are not the behaviour of a respectable young woman and her public physical contact with Thornton leaves her open to allegations of immorality or at the very least 'forward' conduct. Margaret further compromises herself when, following her mother's death, she is seen in public with her brother. Unaware of Frederick's identity, Mr Thornton is severely vexed when he sees Margaret's open display of affection towards another man and grapples with feelings of jealousy and distrust:

> He was haunted by the remembrance of the handsome young man, with whom she stood in an attitude of such familiar

> confidence; and the remembrance shot through him like an agony, till it made him clench his hands tight in order to subdue the pain . . . It took a great moral effort to galvanise his trust – erewhile so perfect – in Margaret's pure and exquisite maidenliness into life; as soon as the effort ceased, his trust dropped down dead and powerless: and all sorts of wild fancies chased each other like dreams through his mind. (270)

Later, when Margaret is forced to lie to the police inspector investigating a claim that she was seen at the railway station when Frederick accidentally killed Leonards, she depends upon her reputation as a lady to repudiate the Inspector's suspicions. She remains calm, poised and dignified, exploiting her class status to dismiss the allegation. Thornton, however, on learning that she has not told the truth believes that she has 'stained her whiteness by a falsehood' (280), which throws his faith in her into doubt. However, as she registers with her impassioned cry, 'I wish I were a man, that I could go and force him to express his disapprobation, and tell him honestly that I knew I deserved it' (309), propriety leaves her unable to explain herself to the man she has come to respect and admire.

Thornton's mother offers a brutal yet incisive analysis of the damage Margaret has done to her good character when she declares, 'These half-expressions are what ruin a woman's character' (313). Acting on her promise to Margaret's dead mother, Mrs Thornton confronts Margaret with her indiscretion, commenting, 'I have thought it right to warn you against such improprieties; they must degrade you in the long run in the estimation of the world, even if in fact they do not lead you to positive harm' (316). While Margaret responds with indignation, Mrs Thornton's warnings reflect society's position on the 'bold' or 'forward' woman and, in spite of her less-than-friendly motives, Thornton's mother is right to warn Margaret that she is providing fodder for gossips. Margaret's difficulties originate partly because she refuses to be constrained by either gender or class roles, treating Thornton as an equal in public and in private. Indeed, towards the end of the novel when her behaviour becomes much more conventional and demure, she is a much less engaging character than the young woman who strides across the working-class slums of Manchester with her head held high.

Maggie Tulliver's reputation is more seriously damaged than Margaret's, following her dalliance with Stephen Guest, even though she draws back from eloping or consummating the relationship. Maggie's drowning spares her the lifetime of social isolation that she could otherwise have expected. Thomas Hardy, however, was rather less compassionate in his treatment of Lucetta in *The Mayor of Casterbridge*. Hardy is never explicit about the extent of Lucetta's 'sin', but her reputation is unquestionably compromised by her relationship with Michael Henchard when he is in Jersey. Lucetta is acutely aware of the vulnerability of her position, which is why she believes, initially at least, that she must marry the mayor. Henchard's rough treatment of her when he announces, 'I come with an honest proposal for silencing your Jersey enemies, and you ought to be thankful' (177) reveals the degree to which she has been devalued, as his language is very different from that of a man wooing a wealthy wife. Lucetta's indignant response in which she protests that she was 'what *I* call innocent all the time they called me guilty' (177) is, as we see later on, irrelevant in the eyes of the Casterbridge community. Coming from the small island of Jersey, Lucetta is vulnerable to blackmail and, significantly, her good name has been jeopardized, while Henchard has not experienced similar treatment. Henchard toys with her good character when he reads extracts from her letters to Farfrae, revealing a cruel awareness of his power over her. The public reading of the letters at Peter's Finger also reveals much more disapproval of Lucetta's conduct than of Henchard's, although this is possibly also because of her superior status within the community.

In Hardy's draconian world, where transgressors are always punished for their sins, Lucetta cannot be allowed to prosper. Like Tess Durbeyfield in *Tess of the d'Urbervilles*, Lucetta dies as a direct result of sexual relations outside of wedlock. Unlike Tess, who is hanged behind closed doors for murdering her seducer, Lucetta's punishment is public and swift. The skimmity ride, while featuring effigies of both Henchard and Lucetta, is clearly designed to punish the woman rather than the man. Although Henchard is out of doors during the incident, Lucetta is at home and a virtual prisoner to the cacophony outside her house. Distressed by the noise and the spectacle, she is naturally terrified that Farfrae will see and that he will no longer recognize her as his wife once her story is known. The epileptic seizure into which she falls leads to death, thus allowing her to evade the type of social mortification she would have experienced had she lived.

Just as Nancy the prostitute in *Oliver Twist* believes that she cannot be redeemed and suffers a violent death at the hands of Bill Sikes instead of seeking a new life, so Hardy's 'fallen' woman, nearly 50 years later, experiences a similar fate. The woman whose reputation had been damaged could not be rehabilitated and communities were generally not forgiving of sexual transgression. As a consequence, those fictitious women who were, like Oliver's mother, 'weak and erring' (415) were either condemned to death by their creators or, very occasionally, allowed to begin new lives in distant lands.

Space and women in the public sphere

Women's occupation of public space was a thorny issue for much of the Victorian period. Not all women who walked the streets were prostitutes, although until the end of the century, finely dressed young women who appeared in public spaces without a respectable escort ran the risk of being considered as such and could compromise their reputations by being seen in the wrong place.

In *North and South,* Gaskell plays with the class and gender politics of the public world. Margaret's visits to Bessy Higgins mark out her altered class status, but they also draw attention to her vulnerability in the public sphere. Unable to afford a carriage or any other 'respectable' form of transport, Margaret walks to her friend's home. While working-class women were forced to travel everywhere by foot in the 1850s, women belonging to the gentry or the middle class seldom walked anywhere. Affluent women might walk in parks, but they would certainly not be seen striding purposefully across a city's slum regions as Margaret does. While the bustling female factory worker was unlikely to be harassed, a well-dressed woman, walking through the streets by herself ran the risk of being misapprehended as a prostitute, so vexed were the politics of public space (see Parsons, 2001: 70). Although Margaret's appearance is too genteel for her to be considered a streetwalker, her presence on the street makes her a type of public property. The girls from the factory comment loudly on her appearance, while the working men leave Margaret feeling threatened and vulnerable:

> [S]he alternately dreaded and fired up against the workmen, who commented not on her dress, but on her looks, in the same open fearless manner. She, who had hitherto felt that even the most refined remark on her personal appearance was an impertinence, had to endure undisguised admiration from these outspoken men. (71)

By appearing on the public streets, Margaret leaves herself vulnerable to the proprietorial gaze, as her body is scrutinized by anyone who cares to look at her. As she learns more about working-class culture, Margaret comes to accept this unwanted attention as something akin to a compliment. However, the fact that she is available to be inspected is a constant reminder of her change in status, while at the same time it also reinforces her physical difference from the stunted, damaged bodies around her.

Elizabeth Gaskell's female protagonists are remarkable for the self-possession and authority with which they move through the cityscape. Gaskell simultaneously took possession of the streets for her characters and for herself, turning the female gaze onto a space that was conventionally coded as male (Nord, 1995: 137). While traditionally only working and 'fallen' women were to be seen on the streets, Gaskell boldly placed her respectable female characters on the public roads. Not only was Gaskell clearing space so that she herself could look at life on the streets, she was also attempting to reconfigure the woman's role so that it would no longer be anomalous or dangerous for a young woman to be on the public roads alone. The most resonant example of this attempt to claim space is when Margaret announces that she will attend her mother's funeral service. Middle-class Victorian women did not attend funerals and when Margaret attempts to account for this fact, she explains, 'Women of our class don't go, because they have no power over their emotions, and yet are ashamed of showing them. Poor women go, and don't care if they are seen overwhelmed with grief' (266–7). Her decision to attend could be interpreted as a recognition of her altered class position, or as a usurpation of a masculine role. However, it also signals Margaret's claim on space and the right to show her grief in public if she so wishes.

Margaret's fearless traversal of the streets makes her an important, transitional character. By the end of the nineteenth century, improvements in public transport, middle-class women's employment in professional jobs and the emergence of department stores (which offered safe destinations for female walkers) meant that women were increasingly able to walk alone without fear of harassment. By the publication of *Dracula* in 1897, Mina Harker is able to cross London on foot and by public transport without a moment's hesitation, thus pointing to the remarkably swift changes that accompanied the onset of modernity.

Masculinity

By the end of the nineteenth century, many people believed that masculinity was undergoing some sort of crisis. The transgressive 'New Man' – an amorphous figure who was at times identified with the decadent or the Dandy, and at others equated with homosexuality – seemed to pose a threat to the future supremacy of Britain. Some of these 'New Men' were condemned simply for their support of the 'New Women', with Eliza Lynn Linton famously declaring in her article, 'The Partisans of the Wild Woman', 'Their morals are the morals of women, not men . . . THE UNSEXED WOMAN PLEASES THE UNSEXED MAN' (quoted in Ledger, 1997: 96).

Jonathan Harker certainly experiences a challenge to his masculinity when he is imprisoned in Castle Dracula. Believing himself to be a model of propriety and monogamy, his self-perception is tested first by the appearance of the three female vampires and secondly by the Count himself. In chapter 3, after Jonathan has disobeyed Dracula's warning and fallen asleep in the old part of the castle, he attempts to analyse his response to the three women who prey on him:

> All three had brilliant white teeth, that shone like pearls against the ruby of their voluptuous lips. There was something about them that made me uneasy, some longing and at the same time some deadly fear. I felt in my heart a wicked, burning desire that they would kiss me with those red lips. It is not good to note this down, lest some day it should meet Mina's eyes and cause her pain; but it is the truth. (37)

While he fears that his desires may be betraying his fiancée, Mina, and the virtue that she embodies, it is clear that Jonathan is drawn to the women, who appeal to his latent yearnings. Although we never learn why one woman in particular makes Jonathan feel uneasy, students in my classes have suggested that this could be because she is Mina's friend, Lucy Westenra. Sally Ledger, in her study of the New Woman, has argued that these women represent the 'real awfulness and terror of the novel' (103) since when they are thwarted in their attempts to feast on Jonathan's blood, they gleefully seize on the baby the Count throws to them, thus reversing the conventional mother/child dependency. The true horror posed by these women is that they do nothing to disguise their desires, making a mockery of the self-sacrificing angel who was the lynchpin of the Victorian home, thus also posing a threat to the type of man who depended upon her.

Dracula's arrival disrupts the novel's focus on heterosexual desire, with the livid Count demanding, 'How dare you touch him, any of you? How dare you cast eyes on him when I have forbidden it? . . . This man belongs to me!' (39). His behaviour towards Jonathan in this scene borders on the seductive, as he looks at his face 'attentively' and whispers softly, 'Yes, I too can love' (39). Jonathan then falls down into a swoon, ostensibly because he is aghast at the women feasting on the baby, but perhaps also because he is unable to face Dracula's desire for him.

It is possible to read the female vampires as proxies for Dracula, given the Count's extraordinary shape-shifting abilities. According to Christopher Craft, 'The text releases a sexuality so mobile and polymorphic that Dracula may be best represented as a bat or wolf or floating dust; yet this effort to elude the restrictions upon desire encoded in traditional conceptions of gender then constrains that desire through a series of heterosexual displacements' (1984: 111). Dracula is responsible for the proliferation of a 'monstrous' female sexuality, which is perceived as ghastly on two levels. Firstly, because the vampish young women who entice Jonathan represent predatory sexual aggression that is at odds with Jonathan's view of femininity, and secondly, because the apparent monstrosity of the women's desires divert attention from the homoerotically charged exchange between Harker and the Count (see Craft, 111). It is possible to develop this interpretation further, reading *Dracula* as an allegorical representation of Stoker's repressed homosexual feelings, focusing on Jonathan Harker's attraction to the vampire and viewing the prowling nocturnal vampire as akin to the gay man driven to pursuing his newly illicit desires in the streets at night (see Schaffer, 1994).

Whatever takes place between Jonathan and the Count is so terrible that Harker is unable to recall it. Mina describes him as 'a wreck of himself', while one of the nuns who nurses him back to health reports that he 'raved of dreadful things whilst he was off his head' (103). When Mina and Jonathan marry, their gender positions are almost reversed; Jonathan is an invalid, whose weakness is emphasized and whose 'quiet dignity' (103) has been lost. It is Mina who has to travel across Europe to rescue her fiancé from the Hungarian convent where he recuperates from his ordeal, while after their return to Exeter she has to coax him back to sleep when he is awakened by 'trembling' nightmares (154). With his fragile health and shattered nerves, Jonathan becomes like one of the sofa-bound heroines of eighteenth-century novels, with Mina having to become the dominant partner.

Jonathan is not alone in his damaged masculinity. None of the male characters we encounter in *Dracula* is a match for the virility of the Count. Indeed, while the vampire is able to drain Lucy's blood by himself, not even Lucy's three suitors working together are able to give her enough, through transfusions, to survive. Fred Botting has gone so far as to suggest that the men degenerate into hysteria, noting that Van Helsing becomes inconsolable after Lucy's funeral, while Arthur sobs uncontrollably when he has driven the stake into Lucy. He goes on to comment that 'male hysteria is a sign of the breakdown and longing for proper social bonds' (Botting, 1996: 152), suggesting that the gender role reversal we see taking place in *Dracula* has had a profound impact on the male protagonists, who yearn for an exclusively male adventure. Certainly, the novel is unusual for the large number of weeping men it contains. When Mina raises the possibility that she too may at some stage need to be treated like Lucy, Jonathan breaks down, flinging himself to his knees melodramatically. The assembled men then all dissolve, as Seward reports, 'We men were all in tears now. There was no resisting them, and we wept openly' (309). Their weeping is in marked contrast to Mina's bravery, thus showing how the Count's influence has challenged gender roles.

Harker's example is an extreme one, but the crisis surrounding masculinity was by no means restricted to fin-de-siècle pulp fiction. Thomas Hardy was in favour of more equal relations between men and women and supported campaigns for female suffrage (see Tosh, 2005: 120). However, Hardy was not averse to depicting some of the challenges that accompanied the reconfiguring of gender relations. His most famous portrayal was in *Jude the Obscure* in which the uninspiring Jude is drawn in by two different types of woman, the sexually assertive 'perfect female animal' Arabella Donn and the nervous, ethereal intellectual, Sue Bridehead (Hardy, 1895: 33). The tensions between the sexes are not quite so pronounced in *The Mayor of Casterbridge* (which, although it appeared in 1886, was set earlier in the nineteenth century. However, the fact that the novel opens with a drunken Henchard selling his wife should alert us to some complexities surrounding relations between the sexes and also to a subtle understanding on Hardy's part of the economics of marriage.

It has been argued that Hardy shows Michael Henchard embarking on a 'pilgrimage of "unmanning" which is a movement towards both self-discovery and tragic vulnerability' (see Showalter, 1979: 102). Henchard – in the first instance, at least – is complicit in his own unmanning, divesting himself of female dependents and turning his attentions to serving the male agricultural community. While readers pass by the sale of his daughter without a blink, the sale of a son would constitute a 'violation of patriarchal culture' (103), thus Hardy shows us the low value placed on women in Henchard's society.

Henchard's masculinity is inextricably bound to his authority, which he believes to be challenged by Farfrae. Having previously been excessive in his support and patronage of the Scotsman, Henchard views Farfrae's popularity and his willingness to contradict him as a threat. The mayor therefore begins to see his friend as a rival and becomes increasingly competitive and combative in his interactions with him. Henchard is mostly an asexual figure, with little time for women, and whose energies are channelled into his business dealings. His initial liaison with Lucetta in Jersey follows a period of illness, which leaves him uncharacteristically vulnerable to female attraction. Later, he revives his interest in marrying her only when he sees that Farfrae is attracted to her. René Girard, in a detailed examination of triangles of desire has argued that relationships of this type are under constant pressure as a result of the competition between those who desire and those who are the objects of desire (1965: 163). However, in Henchard's case the triangle is complicated first by his *lack* of sexual desire and secondly by the fact that he desires to *be* Farfrae, rather than to marry Lucetta. This is not to suggest that Henchard is able to articulate this longing. Indeed, his conduct towards his opponent is unnecessarily aggressive and dominant, while he is threatening in his interactions with Lucetta.

Henchard connects demonstrations of power with manliness and one of the most resonant examples occurs in chapter 15 when he forces Abel Whittle to go to work without his breeches. When he is asked to explain his semi-naked state to Farfrae, Abel declares, 'I shall kill myself afterwards; I can't outlive the disgrace' (99). Farfrae instantly understands the humiliation that Abel will experience and sends him home to change, with the significant directive, 'come to wark like a man' (100). He understands that Henchard's punishment will strip (or perhaps 'whittle') away Abel's masculinity and he also sees that the mayor is abusing his power over an underling. Henchard perceives this intervention as a direct challenge and his subsequent conduct towards Farfrae is sulky and confrontational. Farfrae himself is increasingly indifferent towards this man who seems bent on his own destruction and in alienating those who care for him, suggesting that he is much more comfortable and confident in himself than the embattled mayor.

Dale Kramer has argued that Henchard is feminized and weakened as the novel unfolds (in Showalter, 1979: 112), just as Rochester in *Jane Eyre* is symbolically castrated through being temporarily blinded and losing his hand. However, there are a number of instances in which the mayor vigorously resists his declining power and status. The scene in which he saves Elizabeth-Jane and Lucetta from a charging bull (chapter 29) is, on one level, an example of his strength and fearlessness as he leaves the mighty creature 'half-paralysed' (206). Yet read symbolically, we might reinterpret the bull to represent the force of Henchard's will, charging at Lucetta and terrorizing her with its apparently unstoppable force. Elizabeth-Jane's pity for the injured bull anticipates the sympathy she will feel for Henchard after his solitary, miserable death. Moreover, the desperate desire to speak with Lucetta that he displays as he carries her to the door is almost a continuation of the bull's rampage. Shortly afterwards, Henchard too is wounded, although unlike the bull the pain he experiences is emotional, rather than physical, as he learns that Lucetta and Farfrae are married. Henchard's virility, having been asserted in his subduing of the bull, is now battered when he discovers that he has demeaned himself by exposing the precarious nature of his business affairs to his rival's wife.

The wrestling match with Farfrae in chapter 38 exemplifies Henchard's attempt to reassert himself over Farfrae, who has by this point become mayor and who has in the previous chapter appeared to welcome royalty in the regalia Henchard would once have worn. Although fighting with one hand tied behind his back, Henchard is still able to win, gasping over Farfrae's body, while threatening his life. For some readers this scene, with its panting male bodies, holds an erotic charge, but what is most interesting about it is the complicated power dynamic. Having asserted his supremacy, Henchard then responds to Farfrae's suggestion that he take his life, 'God is my witness that no man ever loved another as I did thee at one time' (273–4). While Henchard may be the physical victor, Farfrae has, from a moral perspective, clearly won and, in spite of his display of brute force, Henchard is left feeling unmanned. He sits and recalls the past, musing like a jilted lover on Farfrae's influence and attractions:

> The scenes of his first acquaintance with Farfrae rushed back upon him – that time when the curious mixture of romance and thrift in the young man's composition so commanded his heart that Farfrae could play upon him as an instrument. So thoroughly subdued was he that he remained on the sacks in a crouching attitude, unusual for a man, and for such a man. Its womanliness sat tragically on the figure of so stern a piece of virility. (274)

Henchard is here, not unlike Jonathan Harker in *Dracula*, disempowered and feminized in the fight's aftermath. His physical demeanour reflects the completeness with which Farfrae has subdued him, and from this point on any power remaining to him begins to decline. He is unable to commit suicide and when he looks down into the water to see a cast off effigy of himself he sees 'the symbolic shell of a discarded male self, like a chrysalis' (see

Showalter, 1979: 112). He then becomes a dependent in Elizabeth-Jane's household, engaging in traditionally feminine activities such as making tea. Ultimately, though, for a character with such a strong investment in manliness, there is little to do but die when that masculinity is taken away. Henchard's death, like the loss of his power, is tragic because he himself is responsible for his downfall.

In spite of his family's best efforts, Tom Tulliver in *The Mill on the Floss* becomes progressively more feminine throughout the novel. When he attends Mr Stelling's Academy, where a regime of hard work is supposed to turn him into 'a man who will make his way in the world' (205), Tom finds himself lacking, both in education and in masculinity. The narrator tells us that 'under this vigorous regime of treatment Tom became more like a girl than he had ever been in his life before' (210) and as Tom's confidence is shaken and he finds himself unequal to the mental challenges handed to him, he is also assigned to household tasks conventionally reserved for girls. Thus, Tom becomes a minder to the Stellings' baby, Laura, and entertains her when her mother is unavailable. Later, when Tom is looking for employment, his uncle complains that the time spent at the academy has 'whitened your hands and taken the rough work out of you' (315), suggesting that his study of the classics has turned him into a fine lady, rather than a man of business.

As Tom grows older, his masculinity becomes bound up with questions of duty and pride, while defining itself against the deformity of Philip Wakem, whom he considers too physically repulsive to be regarded as a real man, or a suitor for his sister. Tom works hard and regains the mill, but he does so at the cost of his humanity. In this respect, he reveals some similarities with John Thornton in *North and South*. Like Tom, Thornton loses his father at an early age (he is a speculator, who commits suicide when his business fails) and works in a draper's shop, saving money and eventually repaying his father's creditors and restoring his family's honour. Thornton is eager to improve himself and engages Mr Hale as his tutor, learning new moral perspectives as well as developing his classical knowledge. Tom Tulliver's character never really develops, though, and he shows the same dispassionate form of justice to the adult Maggie as he did when they were children. As a result, Thornton is able to face the failure of his business with 'inherent dignity and manly strength' (429), and wishes to cultivate 'some intercourse with the hands beyond the mere "cash nexus"' (431), having learned from Margaret that his workers are more likely to cooperate in a climate of mutual understanding. Tom, though, is never able to move beyond his stern sense of the distinction between right and wrong, so that when Maggie is compromised by her relationship with Stephen Guest, Tom's view is that the worst that could happen would be 'not death, but disgrace' (611).

The gentleman

For the mid-Victorians, questions of masculinity were often entwined with debates about what it meant to be a gentleman. In a world where fortunes could be made or lost overnight, manners and breeding became important yardsticks for assessing where people had come from and whether or not they had the 'correct' background to accompany their wealth. As Robin Gilmour has observed, the Victorians attempted to redefine the gentleman and tapped into an 'agreed cultural goal, which facilitated the incorporation of a new élite within the old social structure' (1981: 167). One no longer needed to be a gentleman through birth (although Oliver Twist still manages, even though he is born in the lowliest of settings), rather it was now possible to *learn* to be one. John Henry Newman offered an extended discussion of the qualities of the gentleman in *The Idea of a University* (1852), combining quiet heroism, patience and belief to encapsulate his ideal:

> He has too much good sense to be affronted at insults, he is too well employed to remember injuries, and too indolent to bear malice. He is patient, forbearing, and resigned, on philosophical principles; he submits to pain, because it is inevitable, to bereavement, because it is irreparable, and to death, because it is his destiny. If he engages in controversy of any kind, his disciplined intellect preserves him from the blunder. (146)

Many others joined the discussion, with Samuel Smiles devoting a section of his famous *Self-Help* to the traits of the 'True Gentleman'.

In *North and South,* when Margaret casts doubt on whether the minor character Mr Morison is a gentleman, Thornton declares that he is not the person to decide on another man's gentility, before going on to ponder the term and its appropriateness:

> I take it that 'gentleman' is a term that only describes a person in his relation to others; but when we speak of him as 'a man' we consider him not merely with regard to his fellow-men, but in relation to himself, – to life – to time – to eternity . . . I am rather weary of this word 'gentlemanly', which seems to me to be often inappropriately used, and often, too, with such exaggerated distortion of meaning, while the full simplicity of the noun 'man' and the adjective 'manly' are unacknowledged – that I am induced to class it with the cant of the day. (164, my ellipses)

Thornton here cuts to the heart of the debate about gentlemanliness and, as John Tosh has so astutely noted, his understanding of the term is 'other-related in the negative sense of being caught up in considerations of status and appearance, whereas manliness has to do with interiority and authenticity' (85). When we first encounter him, Thornton seems all too concerned with wealth and status, and part of Margaret's struggle is to reconcile his abrupt Northern manners and approach to business with her Southern model of what constitutes a respectable gentleman. Thornton's masculinity is challenged at several points in the novel, including when Margaret uses her body to shield him and when his business fails. Nevertheless, his willingness to adapt and his patient regard for Margaret (particularly when he mistakes her brother Frederick for another suitor) show him to be a true gentleman.

Dracula and wealth

In his important study *Signs Taken for Wonders* (1983), Franco Moretti presents an intriguing reading of *Dracula,* interpreting the Count as type of aggressive foreign currency speculator who threatens to flood the London market with his foreign gold after a long period of recession. Dracula's position as an aristocrat is irrelevant – he is 'the Count' because of his propensity to accumulate capital. Moreover, the fact that he spurns servants and declines to be a conspicuous consumer of commodities is, Moretti argues, evidence that he has rejected the pleasure-seeking ways of the aristocracy. Dracula's mission to populate the world with vampires is, Moretti suggests, evidence of his similarity to capitalism, as he expresses it, 'Like capital, Dracula is impelled towards a continuous growth, an unlimited expansion of his domain: accumulation is inherent in his nature' (1983: 91). Moretti goes on to interpret the Texan, Quincy Morris, as a vampire ally of Dracula's, who is killed for turning against him.

Although not every reader will be convinced by Moretti's Marxist interpretation of the novel, *Dracula* is a text that is deeply concerned with money and its value. Castle Dracula is so filled with gold that when Jonathan is searching for a key in order to escape, he stumbles upon a heap of it, some of which he steals (51–3). Later, when Dracula is in London, Jonathan Harker stabs him, but instead of blood gushing everywhere, Dracula's body seems to spill money instead:

> [T]he point just cut the cloth of his coat, making a wide gap whence a bundle of bank notes and a stream of gold fell out. The expression of the Count's face was so hellish . . . The next instant, with a sinuous dive he swept under Harker's arm ere his blow could fall, and, grasping a handful of the money from the floor, dashed across the room and threw himself at the window . . . Through the sound of the shivering glass I could hear the 'ting' of the gold, as some of the sovereigns fell on the flagging. (306)

A number of critics have commented on the fact that Dracula 'bleeds' money in this scene, noting that 'at a time of critical danger, the vampire grovels on the floor for money' (see, for instance, Halberstam, 1995: 261). Halberstam interprets Dracula as a type of miser, hoarding wealth and seeing it as a type of lifeblood to be used only for attack. This reading downplays Dracula's outlaying of wealth to purchase land and property in London, which is a securely middle-class strategy. Halberstam, however, sees the bleeding of gold as one more signifier of the vampire's monstrosity, drawing parallels between his excessive wealth and his equally extreme sexuality. Furthermore, she argues that while Dracula abuses his gold, those involved in hunting him spend their wealth appropriately in order to protect themselves.

Towards the end of the novel, Mina Harker writes in her diary of the 'wonderful power of money' continuing to ask, 'What can it not do when it is properly applied; and what might it do when basely used!' (356). Mina's question here suggests that there are correct and incorrect ways of spending, insinuating that Dracula's stockpile of ancient family gold is not being properly spent. The Harkers, though, in spite of their avowed commitment to making their own way, are mostly seen spending other people's money; they are 'adopted' by Jonathan's employer who pledges to leave them everything, while their campaign against the vampire is funded by Lord Godalming. The fact that money is available to them, however, enables the Harkers to assert themselves in the face of danger and places them in sharp contrast with the impoverished characters of the industrial novel, who can do nothing to help themselves. *Dracula* shows us that money can provide agency, while the mid-Victorian novel warns us of the fleetingness of wealth, often juxtaposing extreme affluence with deplorable poverty as a veiled warning to readers of the precarious nature of their good fortune.

The colonies

In the early years of Victoria's reign the Empire was, as Janet C. Myers helpfully expresses, 'pushed to the edges of the novel's range of vision' (4). When colonies feature in novels in the early years of the nineteenth century, they are usually 'offstage', either as sources of great fortunes or as helpful places to which problematic characters can be banished. In *Oliver Twist*, for example, Mr Brownlow disappears from the plot when he travels to the West Indies to learn more of the mystery surrounding the evil Monks and his connection to Oliver. Equally, the Artful Dodger is 'booked for a passage out' (329) and transported as a prisoner to Australia when, towards the end of the novel, he is caught stealing a snuff box.

Charlotte Brontë's writing shows a similar, peripheral engagement with the Empire, although her plot involves more sustained attention than that of *Oliver Twist*. *Jane Eyre*'s imperial subplot includes anecdotes about characters' past lives beyond British shores. Thus, we learn that Mr Rochester's first wife, the 'madwoman' Bertha Mason, is a Creole from Jamaica. Her alleged insanity is presented as a result of her mixed race and the intemperate climate in which she has been raised. When Rochester is forced to explain his history to Jane (following their aborted wedding ceremony at which it is revealed that the first Mrs Rochester is still living), he contrasts the oppressive intensity of the tropical weather with the cool, calming European breeze:

> The air was like sulphur-steams – I could find no refreshment anywhere. Mosquitoes came buzzing in and hummed sullenly round the room; the sea, which I could hear from thence, rumbled dull like an earthquake – black clouds were casting up over it; the moon was setting in the waves, broad and red, like a hot cannon-ball – she threw her last bloody glance over a world quivering with the ferment of tempest. I was physically influenced by the atmosphere and scene, and my ears were filled with the curses the maniac still shrieked out; wherein she momentarily mingled my name with such a tone of demon-hate, with such language! – no professed harlot ever had a fouler vocabulary than she: though two rooms off, I heard every word – the thin partitions of the West India house opposing but slight obstruction to her wolfish cries. (271)

Here Bertha's madness is clearly equated with the weather, as is Rochester's mood. Entertaining suicide as the only escape from his miserable marriage, Rochester is prevented from this rash act by the wind blowing in from Europe, urging him to return home and begin his life afresh. Rochester believes that he can leave the colonies behind him, but in fact his overseas exploits catch up with him and he is forced to keep Bertha with him in England. Brontë here shows that far from being a subplot, the imperial narrative will continue to thrust its way to the surface in an apparently domestic novel.

Jane herself explicitly rejects the colonial plot when she refuses to travel to Calcutta as the wife of her cousin, St. John Rivers. Her decision is consistent with the contrary feistiness of Jane's character, but it also reflects Brontë's more general discomfort with the constraints of realist writing. She declines to accept the trite, conventional ending assigned to many Victorian heroines and explicitly pits herself against conventional closure. St. John, with an eye on propriety, invites Jane to travel to India with him as a missionary, but will only do so if she agrees to be his wife. Although the pair are cousins, St. John insists that for the sake of appearances they must be married, suggesting that if they are not, then their authority as missionaries will be compromised.

Jane's response to St. John's businesslike proposal of marriage not only reflects her romantic nature, but also her refusal to be governed by a man. She identifies St. John's 'hardness' and 'despotism', noting to herself, 'I felt his imperfection, and took courage. I was with an equal – one with whom I might argue – one whom, if I saw good, I might resist' (358). Jane's comments here reveal her continued belief in the possibility of romantic love, in spite of the wrong Mr Rochester has done in attempting to marry her bigamously. Her comments, as she continues, however, suggest a broader rejection of the colonial ending and of the self-repression that would be required of her as Rivers' wife. Jane knows that 'if I go to India, I go to premature death' (356), acknowledging that the regime of hard work and duty ahead of her, combined with heat and disease, will take their toll on her life. Jane's cousin, Diana, reflects the unsuitability of this plot twist when she declares, 'You are much too pretty, as well as too good, to be grilled alive in Calcutta' (366). When Jane considers St. John's characteristically austere, loveless proposal, she figures herself as an Indian widow, engaged in the practice of sati, commenting, 'If I *do* go with him – if I *do* make the sacrifice he urges, I will make it absolutely: I will throw all on the altar – heart, vitals, the entire victim' (356). Thus, although she rejects the colonial resolution, she is clearly drawn to Indian culture and allows it to infuse her language and imagination.

By the end of the century, emigration plots were dwindling as writers became more sceptical about the benefits of exiling their characters to foreign lands. Hardy's Donald Farfrae never actually goes through with his plan to emigrate to America and although Michael Henchard briefly imagines that he will banish himself, he never does so. After 'buying' Susan Henchard, the sailor Newson takes his family to Canada for some time, but they then return to the mother country as Susan never quite manages to settle overseas. While the Empire was a place of promise to many in the nineteenth century, the colonial ending did not always provide closure. Some who travelled to the Empire in search of new lives discovered that they simply did not have the necessary skills or stamina to prosper in countries that were still developing. Others could simply not be compelled to remain overseas and, increasingly, the nineteenth-century novel reflected contemporary concerns surrounding the returnee.

Those who returned did so for a diverse range of reasons. Some were disappointed with the somewhat basic living standards in newer colonies like Australia, others couldn't cope with the climate, or just missed their homeland. Dickens was particularly concerned with those who returned and a number of his novels (including *Dombey and Son*, *Nicholas Nickleby*, *David Copperfield* and *Great Expectations*) feature characters who gravitate back to England after spending time overseas. The evil Monks in *Oliver Twist* is one such example, returning from the West Indies to rob Oliver of his rightful inheritance. Elizabeth Gaskell also examines the dangers surrounding the returning character through her depiction of the mutineer Frederick Hale's clandestine visit to his dying mother in *North and South* (see Morse, 2011 for an excellent, sustained discussion of Frederick's act of mutiny).

In the final years of the century, as Britain's colonial policy became increasingly aggressive, particularly in Africa, concerns about 'reverse colonization' were heightened. Stoker's *Dracula* embodies many of these anxieties, representing the terror inspired by a foreign body gravitating to the imperial centre. Although primarily a horror story, *Dracula* can also be read as an invasion narrative, reflecting late-Victorian imperial panic and anxieties about immigration from Eastern Europe. Stephen D. Arata has argued that the novel speaks to fin-de-siècle concerns about British decline and, noting the popularity of reverse-invasion stories (for instance by Conan Doyle and Rider Haggard) at the end of the nineteenth century, he suggests that *Dracula* is a product of 'cultural guilt' (Arata, 1990: 623). Noting Van Helsing's strong investment in the idea of Dracula as a type of savage or degenerate, Arata contends that he represents a concern with the Empire that is central to the Irish Stoker's fiction. When explaining Dracula's retreat, Van Helsing uses the language of conquest, remarking, 'So he came to London to invade a new land. He was beaten, and when all hope of success was lost, and his existence in danger, he fled back over the sea to his home' (383).

High Victorianism thus gave way to a climate of panic, reflecting a broader fear that British imperial and financial dominance was under threat. *Dracula* thus reflects a turning point in Britain's fortunes and a growing anxiety about how the rest of the world perceived and engaged with the imperial centre.

Endings and generic subversions

As I discussed in the section dealing with the 'problem of ending' in Part One, the rise of realist writing led to an established set of conventions designed to satisfy readerly demands for resolution, which often made the endings of novels seem somewhat contrived. However, by the 1840s a growing number of writers were resisting the impulse to exile characters overseas or to marry them off, just for the sake of pulling narrative threads together. Novelists including Dickens, George Eliot and Charlotte Brontë began to explore the creative possibilities offered by an ending that did not pander to the demands of the literary marketplace and found increasingly creative ways of combining the need to conclude a story with engaging forms of closure that resisted the 'stock' endings of marriage, death, emigration and inherited wealth.

At the end of *Jane Eyre,* Brontë refutes the convention of marrying her heroine off to the most conventionally handsome character. Jane's rejection of St. John Rivers' pragmatic offer of marriage is characteristically feisty as she resists the demands of 'duty' her culture imposes upon women and rejects her icy suitor's cold, calculated advances. Her initial consideration of the offer is unconventional and at odds with the response expected of a well bred woman of the nineteenth century:

> Alas! If I join St. John, I abandon half myself: if I go to India, I go to premature death. And how will the interval between leaving England for India, and India for the grave, be filled? Oh, I know well! That, too, is very clear to my vision. By straining to satisfy St. John till my sinews ache, I *shall* satisfy him – to the finest central point and farthest outward circle of his expectations. If I *do* go with him – if I *do* make the sacrifice he urges, I will make it absolutely: I will throw all on the altar – heart, vitals, the entire victim. He will never love me; but he can approve me; I will show him energies he has not yet seen, resources he has never suspected. Yes: I can work as hard as he can; and with as little grudging. (356)

Jane's words here distinguish her from her more compliant literary predecessors and point to a psychological complexity that will allow her to consider an almost masochistic surrender to Rivers, albeit in the somewhat gruesome terms of a human sacrifice.

Jane is so unconventional that she is willing to entertain the idea of travelling to India as an unmarried assistant, regardless of the potential for scandal that such an action would hold. Given Jane's strength of character and nonconformity, we as readers would feel cheated if she were to give way to St. John's attempts to wear her down and to make her agree to a loveless marriage. A woman who makes comments like 'I will give the missionary [i.e. St. John] my energies – it is all he wants – but not myself' (357) cannot be married off to a heartless, but classically attractive hero-figure. In a different type of novel, she might gradually bring Rivers to love her through her great virtue and guidance, but Charlotte Brontë's heroines are too interestingly awkward to submit to such a clichéd form of closure.

When Jane finally does get her man, after she receives a curious telepathic message from him, it is on terms that sit uncomfortably within the framework of the typical romance plot. In spite of his attempts to lure her into a bigamous marriage, Jane has never ceased to love the ugly, gruff Mr Rochester, who is now conveniently single, following the opportune death of his first wife, the 'madwoman', Bertha Mason. The fact that Rochester has been temporarily blinded in his attempts to save his wife makes him a much less desirable 'catch' than he was earlier in the novel, as does the fact that he has lost an arm. His magnificent home, Thornfield, has been reduced to a ruin and he now lives in seclusion, a much more humble figure than the Byronic hero of the novel's early chapters. He describes himself to Jane as, 'A poor blind man, whom you will have to lead about by the hand . . . A crippled man, twenty years older than you, whom you will have to wait on' (392) and this self-portrait is distinctly at odds with conventional Victorian masculinity. As the novel closes, we see Jane safely ensconced at Ferndean Manor – the home that was previously regarded as an unsuitable retreat for the first Mrs Rochester – married to Mr Rochester and the mother of his children. Yet, as readers, we might feel uncomfortable that Jane is to be hidden away from society, as though she were an illicit mistress, rather than a wife.

Charlotte Bronte, then, chooses to give her readers the marriage plot that her novel has been resisting, but subverts our expectations of what a happy ending might look like. In her later novel *Villette* (1853) she went a step further, tantalizing readers with a highly ambiguous ending and allowing her complex and difficult heroine to withhold information and manipulate our expectations.

In *The Mill on the Floss*, George Eliot takes the 'problem of ending' a step further and demonstrates the difficulties involved in providing a satisfactory resolution for a character like Maggie Tulliver who is ahead of her time. Maggie's intelligence, her inability to conform and her resistance to domestic entrapment mean that there are very few options available to her after she has compromised herself by absconding with her cousin's fiancé, Stephen Guest. Having herself lived with her partner George Henry Lewes outside of wedlock (Lewes was unable to obtain a divorce from his wife, Agnes), Eliot was all too aware of the stigma surrounding women who chose to live in 'sin' and seems to have been unwilling to surrender her heroine to such a fate. While Maggie could eventually have achieved respectability if she had quietly married Guest (who is believed to have been her seducer), the fact that she chooses not to means that she either cannot return home or, if she does so, she will be treated as an outcast. While some readers feel that Eliot takes 'the easy way out' by drowning Tom and Maggie, her decision to do so is entirely consistent with the type of Darwinian imagery she deploys throughout the novel to describe people and places. The Tulliver children simply do not fit with the world they inhabit – Maggie's intellect and apparent 'fallenness' will render her a perpetual outsider, while Tom is simply not astute enough to be able to make his living in the emerging capitalist society.

While Dickens provides a fairly straightforward happy ending in *Oliver Twist*, it is perhaps a conclusion that tries a little too hard. Oliver's life has been significantly improved through the establishment of his true, middle-class identity as the son of Agnes Fleming. With Mr Brownlow and the Maylies as his protectors, Oliver's future is secure, but the boys he left behind in Fagin's lair and back in the workhouse face a significantly more precarious existence. The fact that Oliver's small sickly friend, Dick, is found to have died when Oliver returns to rescue him at the end of chapter 51 reminds the reader – although the narrator does not linger over it – of the many thousands of poor children who do not have benefactors to save them from the misery and abuse of parochial 'charity'. The next chapter shifts its focus to Fagin's last night alive so that the fate of the less fortunate orphans is not examined in any detail. The reader's final vision of Oliver shows him learning and growing under Mr Brownlow's care, but the novel's final lines pertain to the parish boy's mother, Agnes, whom the narrator imagines as a ghost, lingering in the churchyard where her body is buried. This final scene sits rather uncomfortably with the novel's realist elements, but it is consistent with some of the other Gothic aspects (such as the melodramatic villain Monks) and points to the transitional nature of Dickens' writing at this point in his career.

By the end of the century, the satisfying ending could no longer be taken for granted, and in his later fiction, Thomas Hardy is highly resistant to this unrealistic mode. Although *The Mayor of Casterbridge* ends with the faithful Elizabeth-Jane finally married to Donald Farfrae, their happiness is marred by both the misery Michael Henchard has caused them in his lifetime as well as the short, bitter will he leaves behind, containing instructions for his burial. Elizabeth-Jane is, we learn, a much more subdued character who lives in a state of 'wonder at the persistence of the unforeseen' (334), which seems to cast a shadow over any happiness she feels. Compared with *Tess of the d'Urbervilles* (1891) in which the central character is executed for murder, and *Jude the Obscure* (1895) in which Jude the anti-hero dies after a series of horrific setbacks. However, we might agree that Elizabeth-Jane's adult life is actually a fairly reasonable conclusion. Hardy is unable to envisage a uncomplicatedly blissful future for a young woman who has suffered from Henchard's bad temper and deception. The fact that Elizabeth-Jane cannot simply be happy, but assimilates this time of suffering into her life, suggests a psychological complexity that makes her character all the more believable.

Reading

Please see the detailed bibliography at the end of this volume for further suggested reading.

- Dinah Birch, *Our Victorian Education* (2008)
- Elaine Freedgood, *Factory Production in Nineteenth-Century Britain* (2002)

- Catherine Gallagher, *The Body Economic: Life, Death and Sensation in Political Economy and the Victorian Novel* (2008)
- Josephine M. Guy, *The Victorian Social-Problem Novel* (1996)
- Mark Knight and Emma Mason, *Nineteenth-Century Religion and Literature: An Introduction* (2006)
- Francis O' Gorman (ed.), *Victorian Literature and Finance* (2007)
- Mary Poovey, *Making a Social Body: British Cultural Formation 1830–1864* (1995)
- Sheila M. Smith, *The Other Nation: The Poor in English Novels of the 1840s and 1850s* (1980)

Research

Oliver Twist

- How convincing is Dickens' depiction of child poverty in *Oliver Twist*? You might consider comparing Oliver with other characters, including Little Dick and the boys who belong to Fagin's gang.
- Pay attention to Dickens' representation of Jewishness. You might also read *Our Mutual Friend* to examine Fagin alongside Mr Riah, the gentle figure who Dickens created to atone for his earlier character's wickedness.
- Consider the ways in which Dickens blends genres (e.g. melodrama, comedy, Gothic horror, realism). Do you think that a single genre dominates or is the novel a fusion of several forms?
- How does Dickens represent communities in *Oliver Twist*? Give some thought to both successful and failed communities and consider the degree to which Dickens' representation of them may be a veiled critique of the Poor Laws.

Jane Eyre

- Examining scenes including Jane's observations of the party that visits Thornfield Hall (chapters 17 and 18, for example) think about how she uses her marginality as a vantage point from which to interpret and manipulate the world.
- Compare and contrast Mr Rochester and St. John Rivers as 'hero' figures. You might consider how they measure up alongside male protagonists from other Victorian novels you have encountered. Think too about which character is more conventionally heroic.
- Read the chapter on *Jane Eyre,* 'A Dialogue of Self and Soul: Plain Jane's Progress' in Gilbert and Gubar's *The Madwoman in the Attic* (I will discuss this study and its importance in the next chapter). Drawing upon the primary text for examples and supporting your ideas with detailed textual analysis, consider the extent to which you agree with their reading of Bertha Mason as a type of double or alter ego for Jane.
- Matthew Arnold famously wrote of Charlotte Brontë that her mind 'contains nothing but hunger, rebellion, and rage' (quoted in Bloom, 2004: 316). Based on your reading of *Jane Eyre,* to what extent do you agree with this assessment?

North and South

- Pay attention to Gaskell's representation of the dangers associated with industrialism. You could extend your analysis by considering whether men and women are equally vulnerable in the workplace and you might find a comparison with Gaskell's earlier novel, *Mary Barton*, to be productive.
- Discuss Margaret Hale's occupation of public space and the ways in which it challenges gender and/or class conventions.
- Write about Gaskell's representation of the North and its otherness. Your response might include a discussion of her representation of Northern culture, speech and customs as

well as a comparison between the vast industrial cities and the quiet Southern idyll.

The Mill on the Floss

- Think about Eliot's use of natural and Darwinian imagery and how she uses it to negotiate class, gender and family politics. You are likely to find the work of Gillian Beer (especially *Darwin's Plots*, 1983) and Sally Shuttleworth (particularly *George Eliot and Nineteenth-Century Science*, 1984) to be helpful in framing your argument and analysis.
- Write about the gender politics associated with education in *The Mill on the Floss*. You may find it helpful to refer outwards to Eliot's essay 'Silly Novels by Lady Novelists' and to discuss the role that fiction played in shaping gender roles.
- Consider the representation of business in the world of St. Ogg's. To what extent does Eliot depict a clash between the pre- and post-industrial worlds?
- Discuss Eliot's representation of different forms of justice (e.g. legal justice, personal justice, natural justice).

The Mayor of Casterbridge

- To what extent is Henchard responsible for his own downfall?
- Consider Hardy's representation of the difficulties experienced by women in Casterbridge. Give some thought to the politics of wife-selling and consider how Hardy treats Elizabeth-Jane and Lucetta in comparison with Susan Newson.
- Discuss Hardy's treatment of the spread of professionalism, contrasting Henchard's business methods with those of Farfrae.
- Thinking about landscape and culture, consider Hardy's representation of the rural and the extent to which the outside world impinges upon Casterbridge.

Dracula

- Looking ahead to Chapter Five, think about *Dracula*'s popularity and why it has been so appealing to the film and popular culture industries.
- Drawing on the novel for examples, consider the extent to which the vampire embodies fin-de-siècle anxieties about issues including class, race, gender and technology.
- Discuss the clash between superstition and modernity in *Dracula*.
- Consider the extent to which *Dracula* is a conservative novel, which seeks to return women to the domestic sphere. Pay particular attention to Lucy Westenra's monstrosity and Mina Harker's conduct before and after her encounter with Count Dracula.

Extended Research Topic

Consider the politics of the family as represented in any combination of the novels above. Leonore Davidoff and Catherine Hall's *Family Fortunes: Men and Women of the English Middle Class, 1780–1850* (1987) is a valuable resource if you require contextual information on the Victorian middle-class family, as is Anthony S. Whol's *The Victorian Family: Structure and Stresses* (1978). Catherine Waters' *Dickens and the Politics of the Family* (1997) offers a highly useful analysis of Dickens' novels, while Mary Jean Corbett's *Family Likeness: Sex, Marriage and Incest from Jane Austen to Virginia Woolf* (2008) includes excellent chapters on Brontë, Eliot and Gaskell. The questions below are intended to provide guidance in structuring and planning your own project, but they are not intended to be a definitive or restrictive list.

- To what extent are 'family values' either challenged or upheld by your chosen texts? If you perceive a threat to the family, identify and contextualize it.
- Compare and contrast successful and dysfunctional families in the Victorian novel.

- Which novels revolve around family secrets and why?
- Consider why the Victorian novel is so closely concerned with the family. You may find Michel Foucault's *History of Sexuality* (volume one) to be of use here if you wish to think about the connections between industrial capitalism and monogamous reproduction (see Chapter Four of this guide).
- To what degree might the family be regarded as a microcosmic representation of society as a whole?

PART THREE

Wider contexts

CHAPTER FOUR

Critical context

There is a wealth of secondary material available on the Victorians, and it would be impossible to do justice to its diversity and richness in a brief section like this one. This part of the book is a starting point for your research, in which I will introduce you to six studies that have been influential in advancing critical debates. I have selected the works because they represent important yet differing ways of approaching the Victorian novel, often using cross-disciplinary approaches to the texts, and although some of the studies are focused around individual authors and texts, you will find that you may be able to apply the critic's argument and approach to other novels. For instance, *Jane Eyre* is not the only novel to be enriched by a postcolonial reading. The plot of *Oliver Twist* involves a colonial subplot that can be elucidated through applying theoretical tools, just as *The Mayor of Casterbridge* can yield different readings to feminists and ecocritics. You should also keep in mind that literary theory is constantly evolving to reflect the priorities and interests of scholars from different backgrounds and cultural positions.

Marxist criticism and the novel

The work of the Marxist critic Terry Eagleton has played an extremely important role in our understanding of class relations, industrial change and commodity culture in the nineteenth century. Eagleton's expertise spans a range of historical periods and his *Literary Theory: An Introduction* (1983) is one of the best and clearest guides to literary criticism. Marxist theorists concern themselves with the material conditions in which texts are written and published, as well as the circumstances of the protagonists. A Marxist approach to a literary text can involve looking at the politics behind the work, class relations or tensions between characters, but it is also concerned with aesthetic issues like form and style. An examination of an author's artistic choices, such as the decision to use symbolism or allegory, can tell us important things about the writer's context, such as whether s/he was able to discuss political questions overtly, or whether they needed to be veiled (see Eagleton, 1976, especially chapter 1).

In recent years, Eagleton has begun to question the value of high theory, in particular voicing his scepticism about postmodernism in his controversial and compelling *After Theory* (2003). Eagleton has published several important works engaging with the Victorian novel, including *Heathcliff and the Great Hunger* (1996), which includes an extended discussion of Emily Brontë's *Wuthering Heights* and the character Heathcliff's possible Irish roots. *The English Novel: An Introduction* also contains a number of extremely accessible and interesting chapters on Victorian novelists, including the Brontës, Dickens, George Eliot and Hardy.

Terry Eagleton's *Myths of Power: A Marxist Study of the Brontës* (1975) has long been regarded as a classic piece of Marxist criticism. Taking an historical approach to the novels of the Brontë sisters, Eagleton examines their works as products of the seismic changes associated with industrialism and the shift to a capitalist economy. He reads the Brontës as transitional figures, growing up in some of the most turbulent times of the nineteenth century. He works to dispel the myth of Haworth as an isolated pastoral idyll, cut off from the horrors of industrialism. Futhermore, he points out that the town contained a number of wool mills and that the sisters would have been exposed regularly to the poverty that accompanied factory work, looking at Haworth's proximity to West Riding and some of the turbulent political demonstrations that went on there during the Brontës' lifetime. Eagleton argues that even if they did not witness them at first hand, the Brontës would, as children, have been aware of machine-breaking and anti-Poor Law riots in their area, while as adults they would have known all about nearby Chartist activity and demonstrations against the Corn Laws.

Looking at their background and focusing particular attention on their Irish heritage, Eagleton considers the genteel poverty in which the sisters grew up and pays attention to their marginalized position as educated young women required to earn their own living. Examining the time the sisters spent working as governesses, Eagleton points to the cultural clash between their 'professional', cultured background and the leisured lifestyle of those who employed them, noting in particular their difficulties in interacting with those who came from 'new', manufacturing money (like Mr Thornton in Gaskell's *North and South*) but who did not have the benefit of an education (11).

In his discussion of *Jane Eyre*, Eagleton offers an examination of acts of resistance, beginning with the doomed Helen Burns, before focusing on Jane. He examines her awkward class positioning as a rebellious woman, forced to submit to the role of governess – making her both a teacher and a servant – and argues that she is split between two selves, one passionate and emotionally needy, the other required to subdue herself and earn her own living. Eagleton pays a great deal of attention to Jane's childhood experiences, examining the many instances in which she is forced to submit to adult authority and reading her as a calmly calculating, almost entrepreneurial character, who values her independence and seeks to perpetuate it.

One of Eagleton's most provocative interpretations is his assertion that St. John Rivers and Jane are remarkably similar characters. He suggests that in his disciplined conduct, ambition and restlessness St. John 'images aspects of Jane's fractured self which must not be denied' (19), arguing that both Rivers and Rochester dramatize a sequence of conflicts between passion and convention and suffering and validation. Eagleton examines Jane's decision to reject Rivers' proposal, commenting on the would-be missionary's 'imperious masculinity' (21) and analysing the curious combination of self-denial and self-advancement that Jane and Rivers share. He attends to the politics of the family and the challenges that 'kinsfolk' pose to independence in Brontë's world, weighing up Jane's need for autonomy against her desire to dominate (30).

Although the majority of the chapters in *Myths of Power* are centred around Charlotte Brontë's work (including an excellent analysis of the class politics of marriage in *Villette*), the study also contains a discussion of *Wuthering Heights* as a novel depicting the decline of the yeoman farming family (the Earnshaws) and the rise of a leisured bourgeoisie (the Lintons), as well as a final section on the often-neglected Anne Brontë and her depiction of social ambition. Eagleton himself registers that his approach to the Brontës does not reflect more recent developments in politics and critical theory. Writing in an introduction to the thirtieth-anniversary edition of his study, he reflects on his lack of attention to gender politics and the representation of women, noting that interpretations that may seem obvious to today's readers were not so evident in 1975. In particular, although he offers some commentary on Bertha Mason as a double for Rochester, Eagleton regrets his lack of attention to feminist issues, especially in downplaying the complex psychology of Lucy Snowe in *Villette*. Nevertheless, *Myths of Power* remains a valuable resource for those interested in the dialogue between the Bildungsroman and the industrial novel. Eagleton asserts in his introduction that 'all novels are political novels' (2) and shows how the spread of a 'work ethic' and belief in the importance of self-help began to shape character both on the page and in the wider world. Other works of interest to students wishing to pursue a Marxist analysis include Arnold Kettle's work (especially *Hardy the Novelist*, 1967) and Raymond Williams' important analyses of the novel and its relation to the industrial (see bibliography). Sally Ledger's *Dickens and the Popular Radical Imagination* (2007) offers an illuminating study of Dickens' political and aesthetic connections to early nineteenth-century radical culture and includes an excellent chapter on *Oliver Twist*, its literary forerunners and its critique of the Poor Law. Registering some of the limitations of a Marxist approach, Jina Politi's 'Jane Eyre Classified' (1982) charts Jane's progress from work to leisure, while Susan Fraiman's *Unbecoming Women* (1983) fuses Marxism, feminism and an analysis of artefacts, including women's conduct books, to examine the female Bildungsroman.

Jane Eyre as an imperialist text: Gayatri Spivak talks back to Gilbert and Gubar

Postcolonial theory has become a highly useful tool for considering the Victorian novel in its imperial context. The pioneering work of Edward W. Said (*Orientalism*, 1978, and *Culture and Imperialism*, 1993) has made it almost impossible to consider Victorian literature without paying attention to the colonies, which most often form a backdrop to novels, either as a distant source of wealth, or a place to which difficult characters can be banished.

A postcolonial approach to the Victorian novel can involve examining representations of the colonies (although they are frequently referred to 'offstage' as in both *Jane Eyre* and *Oliver Twist*) and colonized peoples. A postcolonial critic will pay attention to voices and silences, noting those characters who are not granted a voice by the author, considering the reasons behind their marginalization and occasionally attempting to reclaim their words. Some postcolonialists are interested in commodity culture and will examine representations of colonial artefacts and merchandise, considering the politics behind these items and their circulation in English culture and society (see, for example, Plotz, 2008).

Gayatri Spivak is an extremely influential theorist, whose work combines feminism, poststructuralism, Marxism and postcolonial criticism. One of her best-known contributions is the essay 'Can the Subaltern Speak?' (1988), in which she examines marginalized figures and the ways in which they have been silenced by those with gender, class or colonial authority. This piece was enormously important in the development of postcolonial scholarship, famously reclaiming the diverse voices of postcolonial subjects and challenging the totalizing approach of Western scholars in approaching and speaking for those who had historically been consigned to the margins. Spivak has explored the tensions between her positioning as a feminist and a postcolonialist, most notably in her work in 'Can the Subaltern Speak?' on sati (the Hindu practice of widow-burning, which was outlawed by British colonial administrators).

Spivak's essay, and the responses it has stimulated over the years, offers an excellent example of the ways in which critical theory develops to unlock new readings of classic texts. Spivak begins by reminding her readers,

> It should not be possible to read nineteenth-century British literature without remembering that imperialism, understood as England's social mission, was a crucial part of the cultural representation of England to the English. (1985: 243)

While this entreaty may be self evident to many students and readers today, when this article appeared in 1985 postcolonial criticism was still in its infancy and not all readers would immediately consider the nineteenth-century novel's imperial context. Indeed, Edward Said took issue with the Marxist critic Raymond Williams in *Culture and Imperialism* (1993) for not engaging with the imperial experience in his monumental study of the novel, *Culture and Society* (65). Spivak's work is engaged in a similar form of revisionism, since it speaks back to Sandra M. Gilbert and Susan Gubar's classic and wide-ranging feminist study of the nineteenth-century woman writer, *The Madwoman in the Attic* (1979).

When it first appeared, Gilbert and Gubar's work presented a radical reassessment of nineteenth-century women writers, arguing for a uniquely female imagination. Along with critics like Elaine Showalter (see, for instance, *A Literature of Their Own*), Gilbert and Gubar refocused interest in the Victorian novel, reclaiming and re-evaluating the voices of women like George Eliot, Emily Dickinson and Charlotte and Emily Brontë, who had been neglected or silenced over the decades. In a chapter dealing with *Jane Eyre*, Gilbert and Gubar discussed the novel's 'rebellious feminism', reading Jane as a character who resists the position of dependency in which she finds herself (338). Following an extended analysis of Jane's fiery temperament, which is unusual for a female character in a Victorian novel, Gilbert and Gubar interrogated Charlotte Brontë's representation of male authority, focusing particularly on the phallus-like demeanour of Mr Brocklehurst, the schoolmaster. However, the most famous re-evaluation offered by Gilbert and Gubar is a detailed close reading of Jane's terror in the run-up to her first, aborted marriage to Mr Rochester, in which they argue that Rochester's first wife, Bertha Mason is an 'avatar' who enacts Jane's secret desires. Bertha is, they assert, 'Jane's truest and darkest double: she is the angry aspect of the orphan child, the ferocious secret self Jane has been trying to repress ever since her days at Gateshead' (360).

In their eagerness to interpret Bertha as a type of evil doppelgänger who empowers Jane by acting out her repressed impulses, Gilbert and Gubar do not always respond critically to the language Brontë uses to characterize Rochester's first wife. They describe her as 'self-destructive and enraged' (383) and write of her hatred and cruelty without always registering that almost all of our impressions of Bertha are channelled through Rochester, even though Jean Rhys' *Wide Sargasso Sea* had attempted to problematize and re-evaluate the character. Too focused on reading Jane as a proto-feminist, Gilbert and Gubar do not probe the possibility that Bertha Mason may have an identity in her own right and that she might be more than a double for the novel's white, privileged protagonist who is, they argue, freed by her death. They do little to examine the forces of patriarchy, which have condemned Bertha to her shadowy existence in the attic of Thornfield Hall.

Spivak intervenes in this debate, arguing that it should not be possible to approach any text from the nineteenth century without giving some thought to how it upheld and reflected imperial values. She draws a parallel between white middle-class feminists and European colonizers to suggest that critics who are too caught up with the fate of white middle-class characters are involved in reproducing and consolidating the colonial gaze. Spivak embarks on a process of what she calls the 'worldling' (244) of *Jane Eyre*, examining Jane's position of privilege in relation to Bertha Mason, but also registering her rebelliousness.

In a detailed analysis of Bertha, Spivak argues that she is 'a figure produced by the axiomatics of imperialism', suggesting that she blurs the boundaries between human and animal, and noting Rochester's construction of the Caribbean and his married state as Hell (247). This animal imagery is not simply a derogatory means of representing a character who has become inconvenient to both the novel's hero and its heroine, but rather it extends into the legal realm and diminishes Bertha's right to be considered as a human being, in possession of the legal and moral rights associated with that state. Put simply, if Bertha is no more than an animal, then she can be imprisoned in an attic without any reservations on the part of the characters, or the reader. For Spivak, Gilbert and Gubar's work falls short in that they see the novel as 'simply replacing the male protagonist with the female' (249). Spivak goes on to examine Jean Rhys' *Wide Sargasso Sea* as a companion piece to the novel (see Chapter Five of this book for a discussion of this reworking of *Jane Eyre*), arguing for the difficulty of extricating the two novels from each other and analysing Rhys' more sensitive treatment of Antoinette, the figure based on Bertha.

Ultimately, Spivak reads Bertha's act of self-immolation during the fire at Thornfield as a type of staging of the act of sati. Jenny Sharpe expands on this interpretation in her fascinating study, *Allegories of Empire* (1993) in which she offers an extended consideration of the many Eastern references in Brontë's novel, as well as a detailed discussion of the 'civilizing discourse' enacted through both the novel and the character, Jane (Sharpe, 1993: 49). More recently, Sue Thomas has produced an extended analysis of the novel (*Imperialism, Reform and the Making of Englishness in Jane Eyre*, 2008), which includes an entire chapter devoted to Bertha and her 'tropical extravagance' (Thomas, 2008: 31).

Not all studies of race are connected to colonialism, and there is a huge body of work dealing with racial encounters in Victorian Britain as well as those out in the Empire. There are a number of studies of Jewishness in literature generally, including Sander L. Gilman's *The Jew's Body* (1991), which addresses the question of Jewish 'difference' through a detailed examination of literary and historical representations of Jews. Gilman's interdisciplinary approach combines psychoanalysis with historical research, close reading and an in-depth knowledge of the history of medicine. Michael Ragussis' *Figures of Conversion: "The Jewish Question" and English National Identity* (1995) is more literary–historical in approach and presents analyses of a number of key Victorian writers and thinkers, including Matthew Arnold, Disraeli, George Eliot and Anthony Trollope. Ragussis' central contention is that British literature and society have depended upon a construction of Jewish outsidedness as a means of defining themselves. Goldie Morgentaler's *Dickens and Heredity: When Like Begets Like* (2000) incorporates a detailed analysis of Dickens' racialized depiction of Fagin, which examines the equation of race with villainy in *Oliver Twist*. Older, but no less useful, studies include Harry Stone's 'Dickens and the Jews' (1959) and Lauriat Lane's 'Dickens's Archetypal Jew' (1958), both of which explore Dickens' mobilization of anti-Semitic stereotypes. Jules Zanger's 'A Sympathetic Vibration: Dracula and the Jews' (1991) discusses Stoker's vampire as a by-product of fears surrounding the migration of Eastern European Jews to Britain at the end of the nineteenth century, focusing particularly on parallels between Dracula and George du Maurier's evil character Svengali from *Trilby* (1895). Zanger considers the novel's attempts to normalize Christianity and to demonize other cultures and religions, while also considering the anti-Semitism behind the press coverage of the Whitechapel murders (see Part One of this book for a more sustained discussion of Jack the Ripper). Christopher Herbert's 'Vampire Religion' (2002) also includes some discussion of *Dracula*'s Jewish subtext, including a reading of the novel alongside William Robertson Smith's 1889 publication, *The Religion of the Semites*, which argues that the work may be read in part as a displacement of religious and ethnic tensions onto a supernatural plot.

Victorian sexuality and surveillance

The work of Michel Foucault has been enormously helpful in discussing Victorian attitudes towards sex and in forcing scholars to re-evaluate their preconceptions regarding Victorian 'prudery'. Volume one of *The History of Sexuality* opens with a rebuttal of received opinions about Victorian sexual repression in which Foucault parodies the demonization of the Victorians. Examining sexuality alongside the rise of industrialism from the seventeenth century onwards, he examines the connections between power, knowledge and sexual identity. At the same time, Foucault pays particular attention to the middle-class family and society's growing emphasis on reproductive, monogamous sexual relations. He asks whether sexual repression is an established historical fact and analyses some of the taboos surrounding the open discussion of sex.

Foucault is especially interested in the marginalization of non-heterosexual forms of sexuality, suggesting that in order to gain control over sex it first had to be suppressed at a linguistic level, so that discussion was no longer encouraged and it thereby became illicit. Foucault examines a well-known piece of late-Victorian pornographic writing, *My Secret Life* by 'Walter', demonstrating the ways in which it resists the apparent injunction against talking or writing about sexual acts and asserting that 'Walter' and those like him expose the lie of Victorian Puritanism.

For Foucault, what is interesting about sex in the industrial age is the way in which it is policed and regulated so that it becomes, paradoxically, both a public and a private issue. Reading the architecture of schools to understand perceptions of childhood sexuality, he argues that, far from suppressing the sexuality of children, the buildings, their organization and their internal regulation confirms its existence and attempts to police it. He also examines the emergence of homosexual identity in the wake of its legal codification and prohibition.

While Foucault did not focus all of his arguments around the Victorians, his writing has been influential for a number of critics concerned with exploring the representation and suppression of various forms of sexuality as represented in the novel. Foucault himself was indebted to the work of Steven Marcus, whose *Other Victorians* (1966) was instrumental in challenging perceptions of Victorian 'prudery' through its wide-ranging analysis of nineteenth-century pornography and erotica.

In recent years, the rise of Queer Theory has expanded our understanding of representations of homosexual identity in the Victorian novel, along with some of the silences surrounding the issue. The work of critics including Eve Kosofsky Sedgwick in her landmark studies *Between Men* (1985) and *Epistemology of the Closet* (1990) has opened up discussions of homosocial and homosexual characterizations, along with concealed plots relating to non-heterosexual desire. Sedgwick examined homophobia in Dickens' novels *Our Mutual Friend* and *The Mystery of Edwin Drood*, as well as female sexuality in George Eliot's *Adam Bede*. Her work, along with that of critics including Judith Butler and Alan Sinfield, has paved the way for queer readings of *Dracula* by scholars, including Christopher Craft and Barry McCrea and work on Dickens and what we would now term gay identity by Holly Furneaux (*Queer Dickens*, 2010) and Susan Zieger ('Dickens's Queer Children', 2009).

There has also been a great deal of interest in childhood sexuality, partly stemming from research into child prostitution by critics like Judith Walkowitz, whose *City of Dreadful Delight* (1992) includes a discussion of female child prostitution at the fin de siècle, with particular attention to Stead's 'Maiden Tribute' articles in the *Pall Mall Gazette* (see Part One of this study for further details about Stead and his context). Writing from positions at odds with Victorian beliefs of childhood innocence, both Larry Wolff (whose work I discussed briefly in part 2) and James Kincaid have paid attention to the sexualization of children in Dickens' writing. Both scholars adopt historicized approaches, with Kincaid in particular arguing that the Victorians perceived children very differently than we do in society today. Kincaid in particular interrogates the term 'innocence' arguing (at times controversially, as in his 1992 study *Child-Loving: The Erotic Child and Victorian Culture*) that the wilful construction of a category of childhood innocence eroticizes the child through fetishizing the idea of purity.

Foucault's work on surveillance in *Discipline and Punish* (1975) has also been extremely important for critics considering surveillance in the Victorian novel. Partly historical and partly sociological in scope, *Discipline and Punish* examines the shifts in imprisonment and surveillance that coincided with the onset of industrial capitalism. He looks particularly at the growing regulation of bodies and thought, examining the parallels between institutions like prisons and schools, and through his discussion of the panopticon (a type of prison designed by Jeremy Bentham to force prisoners to regulate their own behaviour for fear that they might be being watched) he has stimulated a range of work on self-regulation and self-surveillance. Critics working on crime fiction have been particularly eager to draw on Foucault's work on self-policing and surveillance, with D. A. Miller's *The Novel and the Police* (1988) offering an excellent example through its study of imprisonment, watching and omniscience in the work of novelists such as Collins, Dickens and Trollope. Sean Grass' *The Self in the Cell* (2003) attempts to move beyond Foucault by looking at individual selfhood and private forms of entrapment, and re-evaluating the function of the prison in works by novelists including Dickens and Charlotte Brontë.

Darwin and the novel: Gillian Beer

Gillian Beer's *Darwin's Plots: Evolutionary Narrative in Darwin, George Eliot and Nineteenth-Century Fiction* (1983) revolutionized the way we approach the Darwinian undercurrent that is often to be found in novels from the 1850s onwards.

Charles Darwin's theory of evolution and the debates surrounding it had an enormous influence on Victorian culture and society, causing a crisis of faith for some and great scientific excitement for others. Ideas pertaining to evolution, particularly the idea of natural selection and what Herbert Spencer would later term 'the survival of the fittest', entered into general circulation among the middle and upper classes. Articles in the periodical press (including *The Westminster Review*, with which Eliot was involved in the early 1850s) debated evolutionary matters. The theological doubts that they raised and the discussions surrounding issues like the biblical account of the Creation offered a number of appealing tropes and metaphors for novelists and poets (see Part Two for a sustained discussion of Darwin's influence on some of the novelists considered in this guide).

Beer's study has recently been reprinted in a third edition, offering an updated preface, bibliography and a new chapter, 'Darwin and the Consciousness of Others', which looks at some of Darwin's early writings and his concern with consciousness across the species. The study's subtitle is slightly misleading, in that it also incorporates substantial discussions of other novelists, including Thomas Hardy and Charles Kingsley, as well as referring to many other contemporaries such as Dickens, Gaskell and Gerard Manley Hopkins. Beer examines the extraordinary imaginative possibilities that Darwin opened up for the Victorian novelist, while also considering *On the Origin of Species* for its literary qualities based on a climate of freer exchange between the disciplines in the nineteenth century. Examining Darwin's expression of his controversial theory, Beer attends to the accessibility of his language and the ways in which he was influenced by the structure and content of the novel in crafting a study that could be read and understood by the educated lay reader. Stylistically, Beer notes, Darwin drew upon the work of Dickens and Carlyle to create a 'prophetic present which leaves no space between us and the future and poises us on the edge of the unknown' (43). She pays attention to the remarkable organization and plotting involved in expressing a set of ideas that for many readers disrupted both their sense of religious stability and their understanding of humanity's role in the cosmic scheme.

Beer explores some of the literary backlash against evolutionary theory, noting the extreme creativity associated with rejection and revulsion by figures including John Ruskin (7 and 41). She also highlights the work of those like Charles Kingsley, who controversially pushed the theory to its limits in *The Water-Babies* (1862–63), where he examined degeneracy and extinction (116, 120–1), as well as the ideas of Thomas Malthus. Malthus' work on population (in which he argued that famine was nature's way of redressing a population imbalance) was a source of extreme controversy for the early Victorians – Dickens, for instance, attacked Malthusian economics in *A Christmas Carol* (1843) through Ebenezer Scrooge's ill-considered suggestion that the poor might be removed to prisons or work houses. Kingsley used Darwin's ideas to take issue with Malthus and was certainly not alone in transposing Darwinian theory into his work. Indeed, as Beer registers, Karl Marx noted that the naturalist's view of the world replicated, and thus reinforced, existing capitalist power structures, such as the division of labour, free market competition and the centrality of the family.

Following her sustained discussion of plotting and language in Darwin, Beer continues to present case studies of novelists whose work responded to or assimilated Darwinian theory, with particular emphasis on George Eliot. Beer makes a clear case for Darwin's influence on Eliot's writing, noting the breadth of her scientific reading and the influence of her partner, G. H. Lewes. She also closely examines Eliot's scientific discourse alongside works like T. H. Huxley's 1869 essay 'The Physical Basis of Life' (142) to consider their shared characteristics.

Beer's discussion of Eliot is mostly centred on her notebooks and her later novels – *The Mill on the Floss* inevitably does not receive as much attention as *Middlemarch* or *Daniel Deronda* because Eliot wrote the first part of it before *The Origin* was published. The later chapters on Hardy incorporate Darwin's later work and argue for a shared pessimism between the two writers (222). Beer scrutinizes Hardy's treatment of natural laws and his assimilation of the doctrine that came to be known as the 'survival of the fittest' into his depiction not just of animals, but also of the rural peasantry. She also makes the important argument that two particular elements of Darwin's work – imperfect adaptation and the pleasure of life in spite of nature's insistence on suffering (232) – provided an important contradiction in Hardy's writing and his treatment of his characters. She continues to consider 'maladaptation' as it is expressed in *Tess of the d'Urbervilles*, although for our purposes here, this idea of failing to develop to the changing world is, as I discussed in the previous chapter, equally significant when examining the character of Michael Henchard in *The Mayor of Casterbridge*. Ultimately, Beer asserts, Hardy, like Darwin, believes in a type of natural balance or restoration, which enables not just survival, but the pleasurable continuation of life.

Beer's work has generated a wide range of responses and continues to inform present-day debates about race, eugenics and class in the Victorian novel. Recent studies that are indebted to Beer include Angelique Richardson's highly useful study of the New Woman, degeneracy and breeding *Love and Eugenics in the*

Late Nineteenth Century (2003) and David Amigoni's *Colonies, Cults and Evolution* (2007), which shows how scientific language informs our understanding of Victorian and present-day culture. Sally Shuttleworth, like Gillian Beer, works at the intersection between literature and science and her book *George Eliot and Nineteenth-Century Science* (1984) provides case studies of Eliot's major novels and includes an important consideration of memory and science in *The Mill on the Floss*. Among her many other works, Shuttleworth has also published the outstanding *Charlotte Brontë and Victorian Psychology* (1996), which includes a chapter devoted to *Jane Eyre*. Finally, George Levine's *Darwin and the Novelists* (1988) builds on Beer's work to offer an extended analysis of Darwin's significance to Victorian novelists, including those who knew about but may not have actually read Darwin.

Mary Poovey, feminism and interdisciplinarity

Mary Poovey's writing spans a range of fields, but she is probably best described as a feminist historian, with a particular interest in economics and literature. Her work on the Victorians began with what is now considered a 'classic' study, *Uneven Developments: The Ideological Work of Gender in Mid-Victorian England* (1988). Focused on mid-Victorian novels, including *David Copperfield* and *Jane Eyre,* and prominent Victorian figures like Florence Nightingale and Lady Caroline Norton, Poovey's approach brings together work on the history of medicine, law and literature. She interrogates the Victorian idea of womanhood, while at the same time remaining acutely aware of some of the pitfalls of modern-day feminist approaches.

Poovey's study is both archival and theoretical, enabling her to bring together material from medical textbooks, the periodical press, pamphlets, letters and parliamentary debates. Her chapter on women and the medical profession includes a discussion of the use of chloroform in childbirth and the difficult politics behind its use. Poovey also opens up the issue of women's sexuality to explore the contradictions between the sexualized and the domesticated woman, considering the distinctions between perceptions of male and female sexual desire.

Uneven Developments includes a substantial chapter dedicated to *Jane Eyre* and the governess trade, which identifies the governess as a haunting figure, whose presence in the Victorian novel was disproportionate to her presence in real life – there were, for instance 25,000 governesses recorded in the 1851 census, compared with 750,000 domestic servants (127). Poovey argues that the governess generated anxiety because she signified social descent, while at the same time resisting it by living on her distinctly middle-class skills and learning. For Poovey, the governess is a subversive figure who simultaneously upholds domestic values while at the same time threatening them. In addition to examining the material difficulties faced by governesses, Poovey also explores, through both *Jane Eyre* and the proceedings of the Governesses' Benevolent Institution, the psychological strain associated with this type of work (in 1847 governesses accounted for the highest number of women in lunatic asylums). She highlights fears associated with the governess' sexuality and the vulnerability and apparent sexual availability of these impoverished women.

Poovey examines employers' attempts to distinguish themselves from governesses, recalling Blanche Ingram's rude dismissal of Jane Eyre. Through an extended discussion of the writer, art historian and social critic Lady Elizabeth Eastlake's review of *Jane Eyre* and *Vanity Fair*, Poovey argues that Jane Eyre's decision to flee the temptations of Mr Rochester's house marks her out as a 'guardian of sexual and class order' (Poovey, 1988: 136). However, looking at the novel as a whole, Poovey identifies a tension in its implicit suggestion that all women are alike. She argues that Jane's work is idealized (not least because we learn little about it) and that Jane is engaged in a process of 'subordinating her poverty to her personality' (137). Interrogating the 'subversive' qualities of Jane's marriage as an expression of female desire, Poovey considers why middle-class women were so afraid of governesses and looks at Victorian calls to professionalize those who taught in the domestic sphere. Women like the former governess Sarah Lewis argued for training and regulation of governess' working conditions and, Poovey suggests, in the process she highlighted the tensions between 'nature' and 'work' that these women embodied. Debates surrounding the development and protection of governesses also, Poovey notes, became tied to broader concerns about the education of girls and their entry into the labour force.

Poovey's later work, *Making a Social Body: British Cultural Formation 1830–1864* (1995), examines novelists including Dickens and Gaskell, but is more concerned with the working classes than *Uneven Developments*. Examining the connections between gender, race and class and the formation of cultural identity, Poovey again moves between literary sources, sanitation reports and other government documents to address the slippage between discourses of unity and the lived experience of marginalized communities. In addition to examining working-class masculinity, Poovey also studies the Irish presence in England (particularly in Northern manufacturing cities, where many sought work to escape famine at home) and the ways in which the Irish labouring body complicated the self-perception of the English working poor.

Most recently Poovey has published *Genres of the Credit Economy* (2008), which examines the infusion of financial language into the novel and other cultural forms. This work is not uniquely focused on the Victorians, beginning in the late seventeenth century to chart the development and influence of capitalism. However, the study ends with a section devoted to literary value and case studies of several Victorian novels, including Dickens' *Little Dorrit* and Eliot's *Silas Marner*.

Poovey is, of course, not the only critic whose work crosses disciplinary boundaries. Regenia Gagnier's fascinating work on the fin de siècle brings together economics, aesthetics and gender studies, while her most recent book, *Individualism, Decadence and Globalization* (2010), offers a riveting analysis of decadence in an international context. Equally, Nancy Armstrong's scholarship (especially *Fiction in the Age of Photography*, 1999 and *How Novels Think*, 2006) crosses conventional disciplinary borders to situate the Victorian novel in the broadest possible cultural context.

Ecocriticism and the novel

Ecocritical approaches to the Victorian novel are becoming increasingly popular as literary criticism attempts to make itself more socially and politically engaged in the face of broad-sweeping natural disasters like climate change and global warming. Ecocritical work is generally cross-disciplinary, and involves the study of how the natural world is represented in both literature and broader culture, often reaching out to consider the clash between humans and nature (see Garrard, 2007, for a comprehensive and accessible introduction to ecocriticism and its application). There are a number of different emphases within ecocriticism, which makes it difficult to generalize about the work that is being undertaken. However, the approach is broadly concerned with landscape, environment and the natural world.

A number of ecocritics are engaged in examining representations of animals as conduits for human characteristics. The historian Harriet Ritvo's work has been an important influence for those working on animals, in particular her *The Animal Estate* (1987) in which she examined parallels between the human and natural worlds. Ritvo engages with movements to prevent animal cruelty, such as the anti-vivisection movement, and also examines late Victorian concerns surrounding rabies, which undoubtedly fed into Bram Stoker's decision to have Count Dracula metamorphose into animals including bats, dogs and wolves. Ritvo considers the ways in which animals were brought to represent marginalized groups, including both the colonized and the working classes, while also examining the rise of the animal companion and the class politics involved in keeping a dog in the home, rather than putting it out to work. In a later study, *The Platypus and the Mermaid* (1997), Ritvo considers the classification of animals by diverse groups of Victorians, and the ways in which they responded to the challenges of evolutionary theory. Ritvo's discussion extends to consider a range of Victorian novels, including the exotic specimens brought back to England by the sailor Will Wilson in Gaskell's *Mary Barton.*

Although Ritvo's work is historical in focus, it has been hugely influential on literary critics, with scholars including Tess Cosslet, Ivan Kreilkamp and Teresa Mangum engaging in extended studies of animals and their representation in the Victorian novel. Many animal scholars are interested in how creatures can be made to express, reflect or absorb emotions that human characters may not be able to register. In an essay on the dog Bull's-eye in *Oliver Twist*, for example, I examined the ways in which Dickens displaced extreme domestic violence aimed at the prostitute Nancy onto Bill Sikes' dog. Arguing that Nancy, Bill and Bull's-eye form a triangular relationship, which is disrupted by the arrival of Oliver Twist, I examined the ill-treatment of both the dog and the prostitute, focusing particularly on Bull's-eye's mediation between the two humans, as well as his apparent suicide at the end of the novel (see Moore, 2007).

While a large number of Victorian novels were set in cities, many of their characters express nostalgia and yearning for the countryside, which was then, as now, viewed as being in peril. Although there has been a great deal of interest in the Romantic landscapes of the late eighteenth and early nineteenth centuries, ecocritical work on the Victorian countryside has lagged behind. This is not to suggest that nobody has paid any attention to the clash between the pastoral and the metropolitan in the past. Indeed, Raymond Williams' *The Country and the City* (1973) outlined some of the tensions between urban expansion and rural community life from a Marxist perspective.

At first glance it may seem as though subjecting Thomas Hardy's novels to an ecocritical reading would produce a fairly predictable result. Williams himself warned, 'It is common to reduce Hardy's fiction to the impact of an urban alien on the "timeless pattern" of English rural life' (200). He goes on, though, to urge readers to examine the external pressures on characters, namely the expansion of the city and the developing capitalist economy. Ralph Pite in an essay entitled '"His Country": Hardy in the Rural' argues for a need to 'disrupt' some of the assumptions we make about Hardy and place (2009: 133). According to Pite, who fuses ecocriticism with globalism, it is simplistic to read Hardy's works as attempts to memorialize 'Wessex' as a type of pastoral idyll. Rather, we should be alert to what he terms the 'genuinely rural', which attempted to resist an invasion of middle-class idealists, 'who were building cottages in the country and both writing and reading books about the delights of rustic life' (134). Pite suggests that readers and critics have been complicit in a fetishization of both innocence and place in relation to Hardy and draws upon his war poetry to argue for a more cosmopolitan reading of his work.

The narrator of *The Mayor of Casterbridge* is, to a degree, complicit in creating a view of Hardy's world as narrow and parochial when s/he says at the beginning of the novel, 'To the liege subjects of Labour, the England of those days was a continent, and a mile a geographical degree' (27). The novel is, of course, an historical novel and so the characters do not move about with the rapidity of the thoroughly modern protagonists of *Jude the Obscure*. Nevertheless, this comment negates the plot's reliance on its characters' mobility. Farfrae has, of course, come from Scotland, Elizabeth-Jane and her mother have been to Canada and back, while Henchard, Lucetta and Jopp all move between the mainland and Jersey. We also encounter a number of itinerant characters, including the old fermity seller who witnesses the wife-selling and later appears in Casterbridge to expose the mayor's crime.

Writing of Hardy's poem 'Geographical Knowledge' (1905), Pite notes that it issues a challenge to the expectations we extend to the rural, asserting that Hardy believed that 'rustic folk are becoming global citizens whether they travel abroad themselves or stay at home' (138) and arguing that love of place is challenged by events beyond the rural community, including war. For Pite, Hardy seeks to confront the outsider who views the countryside and its inhabitants in a partly condescending and partly idealized manner. Indeed, Pite goes so far as to argue that interpretations of Hardy's writing that privilege the rural reveal more about our contemporary nostalgia for the countryside and what we regard as a 'simpler' way of life that they do about the nineteenth century. He continues to interrogate the notion of rusticity and to take issue with other, less complicated ecocritical readings of Hardy, including work by Jonathan Bate (*The Song of the Earth*) and Lawrence Buell (*The Future of Environmental Criticism*), which essentialize Hardy by tying his work too closely to place, and by overstating their claims for the insularity of his world. For Pite, the rural remains a compelling topic, but he argues that readers must be more willing to think beyond the binary of country *versus* city to understand the cultural exchange between the urban and the rural.

New directions for Victorian studies

According to Miles Taylor, Victorian studies is in a healthy 'state of flux' in which the discipline is redefining itself as scholars find new directions and approaches (Taylor, 2004: 9). Joanne Shattock points out that as the field expands to incorporate more and more authors whose works are being rediscovered or reclaimed, our present understanding of Victorian studies will alter. She remarks that some writers, including Dickens, Eliot and the Brontës, will continue to be regarded as of central importance, but suggests that more generally interests will expand and shift (Shattock, 2007: 1283). One reason behind this change is the widening of access to nineteenth-century periodicals that has been facilitated by advances in digital technology. However, cross-disciplinary and interdisciplinary approaches are also changing the ways we engage with the nineteenth century and its novels. Sue Lonoff has commented that, whereas in the past 'Victorian literature' referred to texts written by those based in England, there is growing interest in the works of those writing under British colonial rule, as is exemplified by Elleke Boehmer's work on the Indian poet and activist Sarojini Naidu (Lonoff, 2002: 175). Cultural studies has expanded the boundaries of the text, so that critics like Thomas Richards are able to analyse cultural artefacts including advertisements and postcards alongside novels. Jay Clayton's remarkable *Charles Dickens in Cyberspace* (2003) makes a number of important connections between Victorian novels and scientific theory and contemporary culture, arguing for 'alliances' across disciplines and integrating the nineteenth century into discourses of postmodernism. At the same time, Victorianists are becoming increasingly politically engaged and working on issues like terrorism (see, for instance, the work of Adrian Wisnicki) and climate change, as exemplified by Upamanyu Pablo Mukherjee's work on natural disasters and imperial culture.

Review

- This chapter explored a range of critical responses to the Victorian novel: Marxist, feminist, queer, ecocritical, economic and postcolonial. It offered readings of a number of influential works in each area, and suggested further readings.
- It also discussed potential new directions for Victorian studies, particularly in the light of cross-disciplinary work and developments in information technology.

Research

- Read Mary Poovey's chapter on governesses in *Uneven Developments*, 'The Anathematized Race', and consider the degree to which Jane Eyre conforms to Victorian expectations of a governess. Consider the ways in which the novel engages with contemporary discussions on governesses and insanity, and pay attention to the ways in which Jane occupies the margins. Jane's account of Blanche Ingram's visit (chapters XVII and XVIII) will be particularly helpful to you here.
- Consider the representation of class relations and/or class tensions in one of the novels we've been discussing – Gaskell's *North and South* in particular offers a number of opportunities to consider cross-class encounters. You might extend this question to address the degree to which class becomes entangled with other concerns, such as race and gender, taking the opportunity to reflect on some of the limitations of a purely Marxist approach to any text.
- Write a critical evaluation of the representation of power in *Jane Eyre*. You might pay attention to the authority wielded against women and children and/or the ways in which institutions (such as schools) uphold existing power structures. You could also consider Brontë's representation of resistance, paying particular attention to Jane Eyre's interactions with Mr Brocklehurst, Mr Rochester and St. John Rivers.
- Using Gillian Beer's idea of 'maladaptation', think about how the characters in either *The Mill on the Floss* or *The Mayor of Casterbridge* have adapted or failed to change themselves to fit with their environments. You might consider the adaptation in economic terms (for instance, think about the distinction between Tom Tulliver and Bob Jakin) or you might think more broadly about issues of social integration (e.g. a comparison between Michael Henchard and Donald Farfrae in *The Mayor of Casterbridge*). Chapter 2 of *Darwin's Plots* will assist you in theorizing your approach to this question.
- Looking at Stoker's descriptions of Count Dracula, consider the extent to which you agree with Herbert and Zanger's

readings of the vampire as an embodiment of fears surrounding Jewish immigration in the late nineteenth century.

- Examine the ways in which the colonies are represented or form a backdrop to the action of one or more novels. You could consider Jane Eyre's refusal to travel to India, Mr Brownlow's travels to Demerara in *Oliver Twist*, or Henchard and Farfrae's plans to emigrate in *The Mayor of Casterbridge*. A more detailed approach could involve looking at the presence of imperial commodities in a novel like *North and South*, where the more affluent characters in the early chapters enjoy a range of imported luxuries from the Empire.
- Consider the ways in which humans engage with landscape and/or animals in the work of either George Eliot or Thomas Hardy. You may find it useful to consult Garrard's *Ecocriticism* before you begin.

CHAPTER FIVE

Afterlives and adaptations

The decline of the Victorians

While Victorian novels are widely read today, their popularity has not always been assured. Towards the end of Queen Victoria's reign there began a revolt against what was perceived as 'high' Victorianism. Late Victorians, including Oscar Wilde, George Bernard Shaw, Edmund Gosse and Samuel Butler, reacted against the earnestness and work ethic they attributed to the mid-Victorians, the value they placed on middle-class culture and their society's emphasis on manners and morals. Wilde in particular sought to satirize mid-Victorian middle-class propriety in plays like *Lady Windermere's Fan* (1892) and *The Importance of Being Earnest* (1895), which ridiculed the propriety that came to be associated with the mid-Victorian period. Many writers and artists at the fin de siècle experienced a sense of belatedness, in that they found themselves daunted in the face of their immediate predecessors' achievements. They expressed their difference in a variety of ways, flouting convention through grittier subject matter (as in the case of George Gissing), decadent content (exemplified by Wilde and his illustrator Aubrey Beardsley), along with the rise of new subgenres, including 'New Woman' fiction.

The novel itself began to change shape towards the end of the century, and while some of these changes were driven by aesthetic values, they were also determined by the demands of the marketplace. Forster's Education Act of 1870, as I noted in Part One, had produced a new generation of readers, who lacked the time to wade through lengthy works. New forms of novels arose to cater to these readers, most notably the adventure narrative, which often focused on some act of heroism in the wilds of the Empire. Works like Rider Haggard's *She* (serialized 1886–87) and *King Solomon's Mines* (1885) were, as I discussed earlier, immensely popular and although aimed at working people and schoolboys, gained popularity across classes. Bram Stoker's *Dracula* offers another example of the sensational adventure story aimed at this new generation of readers and is staggeringly different from the mid-Victorian realist novel. Not everyone was happy about the shift from three volumes to one, though, and authors who had relied on the revenue from sales of triple-decker novels struggled to adapt to changes in the market. The novelist George Gissing, who regarded himself as a successor to Dickens, painted a particularly grim picture of the tribulations attached to the shortening of the novel in his portrait of hack writers, *New Grub Street* (1891).

The attempt to move away from what Henry James called the 'loose baggy monsters' that were the three-volume works was picked up by the Modernist writers in the early twentieth century. Their doctrine was to 'make it new' and writers including the biographer Lytton Strachey and the novelists Vita Sackville-West and Virginia Woolf had no time for what they regarded as the stuffy staidness of their immediate predecessors. Virginia Woolf famously argued in her essay 'Mr. Bennett and Mrs. Brown' that 'on or about December 1910 human character changed' (Woolf, 1924: 38) and she and fellow Modernists like Strachey sought to disassociate themselves from their Victorian heritage by radically recasting art and prose to reflect the dynamism and velocity of the twentieth century. In doing so, they wilfully misrepresented the progress and extraordinary change that had characterized the Victorian period, particularly downplaying the inventiveness of late Victorians like Wilde, Hardy and Stoker. They also, as Steve Ellis points out in *Virginia Woolf and the Victorians*, downplayed their own identities as Victorians, conveniently eliding the fact that they had all been born in the twilight years of the nineteenth century (Ellis, 2007: 11).

One of the most outspoken reshapers of the Victorian legacy, Woolf was famously connected to a large number of very well-known Victorians (including the novelist W. M. Thackeray and the photographer Julia Margaret Cameron, as well as her own father, Sir Leslie Stephen), and it is likely that she was intimidated by the achievements of her immediate ancestors. She regularly satirized the Victorians in both her novels and her literary criticism, famously reimagining the colossus-like mid-Victorian novelists such as Dickens and Trollope as Eusebius Chubb. This mocking portrait of a novelist has a wife 'in the throes of her fifteenth confinement' and, 'after writing thirty-five folio pages one morning "all about nothing"', sits down to write a literary passage as flabby as his name and then lies his head in a gas oven in a desperate act of resistance against the damp heaviness of his age (Woolf, 1928: 220). Woolf's irony was deeply self-conscious, in that she herself recognized her own need to cut the Victorians down to size (see Moore, 2008, for a more detailed discussion of the Modernists' reinvention of the Victorians).

While it would be wrong to suggest that Woolf and the Bloomsbury group are somehow solely responsible for a decline of interest in the Victorians in the early twentieth century, their attitudes reflected a wider rejection of the previous century that was partly connected to the horrors of World War I, which was widely perceived as a conflict inherited from the Victorians. Those who came after the Victorians wanted to present themselves as progressive, energetic modernizers and, in order to do so, they downplayed the extraordinary achievements of their immediate forebears, often with biting satire. The backlash against Victorianism continued until after the Second World War, when campaigners (including the poet and founder of the Victorian society, John Betjeman) began to raise public interest in the nineteenth century, partially in response to the obliteration of Victorian buildings during the bombing of British cities. The Festival of Britain in 1951 evoked nostalgia for the 1851 Great Exhibition at the Crystal Palace and celebrated the Victorian past, reanimating interest in the previous century. Meanwhile, the founding of the Victorian Society in 1958 led to prominent public campaigns to preserve Victorian architecture. While Victorian 'taste' had been a subject for ridicule in the early years of the century, by the 1950s people were attempting to understand the Victorian aesthetic, in the process exemplifying James Laver's law of the 'gap in appreciation', whereby it takes the passing of three generations before a style can be understood and valued again. In Laver's words, 'It seems to be a law of our own minds that we find the art forms of our grandfathers amusing and those of our great-grandfathers attractive and even beautiful' (in Taylor and Wolff, 122).

The Victorians around us

The presence of Victorian buildings and monuments on the streets – not only in Britain, but throughout her former colonies – might partly explain why, as readers, we are drawn back to nineteenth-century writing and why contemporary novelists are so captivated by the idea of the Victorian novel as a text to be reimagined and reworked. The Victorian tourist experience goes beyond the buildings that the Victorians left behind, however. Those who are keen to learn more about the sufferings of Oliver Twist and orphans like him are able to visit the National Trust's workhouse in Southwell, Nottinghamshire, whose website boasts that it is 'the best-preserved workhouse in England' and offers opportunities for tourists to play the 'master's punishment game'. Those who desire total immersion in the Dickensian experience can elect to visit 'Dickens World' in Chatham, Kent where educational experiences sit alongside the 'Haunted House of 1859' and a sequence of 'fright nights'. Holidaymakers regularly undertake pilgrimages to the Brontë Parsonage Museum in Haworth, Yorkshire, to see for themselves where the Brontë sisters grew up. Others flock to Whitby Abbey for the 'Dracula Experience', while the more intrepid are able to take a Dracula-themed tour to Transylvania, following in the footsteps of the original Prince Vlad Dracula, visiting vaults and even a 'chamber of fears and tears'. The dauntless visitor to London can, furthermore, participate in any number of grisly 'Jack the Ripper Tours', tracing the path of destruction left by the elusive serial killer.

Victorian dramas and comedies are frequently revived on the stage, with Oscar Wilde remaining a firm favourite. Classic Victorian novels have also been transformed into smash-hit musicals like Lionel Bart's *Oliver!* (1960), which was adapted for the screen in 1968, and which experiences regular revivals in the West End and on Broadway. In recent years, Andrew Lloyd Webber has transformed Wilkie Collins' 1860 sensation novel *The Woman in White* into a musical (2004), while less well-known adaptations include Roger Holman and Simon May's *Smike* (1973), a musical based on the early chapters of Dickens' *Nicholas Nickleby*, and Cliff Richard's extraordinary adaptation of *Wuthering Heights*, *Heathcliff* (1997). The Victorians have even made their way into reality TV through the BBC talent show *I'd Do Anything* (2008), in which a group of young boys competed for the part of Oliver Twist in a revival of Lionel Bart's *Oliver!*, while young female singers vied for the role of Nancy. The show was highly popular, with members of the public and a panel of judges working in combination to select the successful performers, and it regularly attracted over six million viewers.

Neo-Victorianism and the classic novel

Of course, it isn't just popular culture that reflects shifts in attitudes towards the Victorians. The Victorian novel has provoked extreme reactions in generations of readers and, as a consequence, it is frequently reinvented and reshaped. Some of these reworkings are tributes to the energy and inventiveness that characterized so many Victorian writers, while others are indictments of nineteenth-century attitudes towards class, race and gender. Today, these novels tend to be known as Neo-Victorian texts, although critics also refer to them as 'historical novels', 'revisions' or even 'updates'. This is not an entirely new phenomenon; the historical novel was a popular genre in the nineteenth century, and writers including Walter Scott and William Morris regularly looked to the past for their inspiration. Nevertheless, the literary world seems irresistibly drawn to the nineteenth century, and it is worth taking the time to consider why that might be the case.

There has been a veritable explosion of Neo-Victorian novels since the 1960s, as previously marginalized groups have sought to regain voices that were silenced by the Victorians. Jean Rhys' *Wide Sargasso Sea* (1966), for instance, is, as I mentioned briefly in Chapter Four, a reworking of *Jane Eyre* that taps into the work of the women's movement in the 1960s in providing the 'mad' Bertha Mason with a voice. At the same time, Rhys also highlighted some of the tensions emerging as Britain's imperial control yielded to decolonization, picking up on Charlotte Brontë's fleeting references to Bertha's Creole identity, which imply that her inherited 'madness' and drunkenness are a result of her 'bad blood'. Rhys reworks the story from Bertha's perspective, renaming her Antoinette Cosway and allowing her to challenge Rochester's version of events. Rhys' 'madwoman' is a much more lucid, charismatic figure than Brontë's Bertha. Robin Gilmour has gone so far as to suggest that Rhys' work, when read in conjunction with Gilbert and Gubar's critical study *The Madwoman in the Attic*, can irrevocably change the way we read and understand *Jane Eyre* (198).

Gilmour offered helpful categories to distinguish between the various forms of Neo-Victorian novels (190). His list is very detailed and worth reading in its entirety, but here are his main categories, along with a brief summary of his definitions:

- **The historical novel.** This type is written from a modern perspective and in a modern voice. According to Gilmour, the narrators of these novels tend not to intervene.
- **Pastiche and parody.** Gilmour describes this as a type of 'ventriloquism' that sometimes applies to a whole novel, but is sometimes limited to passages like letters, poems, diaries or other extracts. Stylistically, the author will try to sound as 'authentically' Victorian as possible.
- **The inversion of Victorian ideology.** This type of novel attempts to subvert Victorian ideas of hero worship by bringing a character who would normally be regarded as a loveable rogue to the fore. Gilmour cites George MacDonald Fraser's *Flashman* novels as examples of this inversion, noting how Fraser undercuts the values at the core of the original novel, *Tom Brown's Schooldays*, and those underpinning Rugby School.
- **The subversion of Victorian fictional norms.** For Gilmour, John Fowles' *The French Lieutenant's Woman* (1969) exemplifies this subgenre, since it combines parody of the Victorian novel with more recent, postmodern narrative techniques, often showing a playfully cavalier attitude towards historical accuracy.
- **The modern reworking or completing of a classic Victorian novel.** A fairly straightforward form. Examples include Rhys' *Wide Sargasso Sea,* which revises *Jane Eyre.*

- **The research novel.** A self-referential form, which registers the academic fascination of the Victorians and involves characters in the present researching the past.

Gilmour continues to note that, 'The period is an inviting one for parody and experimentation just because it is so seemingly solid and so unselfconscious in the expression of its official attitudes', suggesting that the Victorians present a challenge to the contemporary writer because they seem so very sure of themselves. So, while a novelist like A. S. Byatt uses her work to express admiration for the Victorians as she does in *Possession* (1990), a writer like the Guadeloupan Maryse Condé addresses the nineteenth-century novel's Eurocentricity in *Windward Heights* (1998), a work loosely based on Emily Brontë's *Wuthering Heights*, which explores issues of ethnicity and outsidedness in much more detail than its original. Indeed, we are endlessly engaged in renegotiating and reconfiguring our relations with the Victorians and our identities as their descendants (see Llewellyn, 2008: 165).

Miriam Elizabeth Burstein in her popular blog 'The Little Professor' has listed 11 tongue-in-cheek 'rules' for those contemplating writing a Neo-Victorian novel, which include:

- All heroes and heroines are True Egalitarians who disregard all differences of Class, Race and Sex.
- Heroines, in particular, are given to behaving in Socially Unacceptable Ways, which is always Good.
- All heroes and heroines are Instinctively Admired by members of Oppressed Populations.
- Any outwardly respectable man will
  - have frequent recourse to Prostitutes,
  - have a Dark Secret, and/or
  - be Jack the Ripper.
- There must be at least one scene set in a Wretched Slum, which will be very Dirty and Damp.

Burstein's 'rules' are particularly helpful in that they help us to reflect on the preconceptions we often harbour about Victorian society, which is frequently represented as secretive and hypocritical by Neo-Victorian novelists. Burstein also, of course, highlights some of the constraints under which our Victorian predecessors were labouring, reminding readers that some issues simply could not be mentioned in a respectable novel.

Seeking to explain the popularity of the Neo-Victorian novel, Gilmour has commented that 'no single set of explanations will do', noting that it could simply be a fashion or craze, or perhaps nostalgia for a time that now appears to have been a simpler one (198). He continues, however, to remark that 'novelists would not evoke the Victorian past if they did not feel that this enabled them to see things in a new or different way' (198). Some Victorian authors are revised much more frequently than others, perhaps partly because of their influence and popularity (classic novels remain widely taught and often still appear on examination syllabi across the globe) or because of their perceived oversights in relation to issues like race, gender and class. Dickens' works have been useful fodder for the revisionists and the range of reworkings spans from gentle parody to outright attack, depending upon the agenda and cultural positioning of the revisionist. Recent reworkings of Dickens' fiction include the Australian Peter Carey's *Jack Maggs* (1997), which explores the Australian identity of a figure based on Magwitch in *Great Expectations* and asks, with some degree of incredulity, why he would ever have risked his life and fortune to return to damp, murky Victorian London. Lloyd Jones' *Mister Pip* (2006) transposes *Great Expectations* to a Bougainville classroom, where it is reworked and reinterpreted once the original text is lost. Richard Flanagan's *Wanting* (2008), which offers a fictional account of Sir John and Lady Jane Franklin's time in Tasmania, includes Dickens as a character and explores his behaviour during the 1850s, when his marriage broke down and he made some of his most controversial statements on people of other races. Dan Simmons' *Drood* (2009) is one of a number of novels stimulated by Dickens' final, unfinished work, *The Mystery of Edwin Drood*. Simmons is less concerned with finishing Dickens' last work than with exploring a range of wild imaginative sources for the surreal imagery that characterizes the perplexingly exotic chapters that Dickens left behind. Likewise, the Brontës – particularly Charlotte and Emily – have spawned a wide range of Neo-Victorian novels by writers with a variety of creative agendas. Patsy Stoneman has devoted an entire scholarly monograph, *Brontë Transformations* (1996), to analysing adaptations of *Jane Eyre* and *Wuthering Heights* across a range of media, including theatre, film, comic books and ballet, as well as the novel.

George Eliot is not revised as often as Dickens and Brontë, although Maggie Tulliver definitely inflects the character Lucinda in Peter Carey's *Oscar and Lucinda* (1988). Eliot, who is supposed to be a friend of Lucinda's mother, is mentioned in the novel, which also draws heavily on Dickens' fiction and Edmund Gosse's famous autobiographical account of his Victorian upbringing, *Father and Son* (1907). Eliot is, in Carey's attempt to deflate what he perceives as Victorian pomposity, 'forty-six years old and bad-tempered with kidney stones' (202) and a disdain for Lucinda's colonial manners. As a child, Lucinda receives a doll sent by Eliot from the 1851 Great Exhibition. In a scene that blurs Maggie's desperate disfigurement of her doll in chapter 4 of *The Mill on the Floss* with her cutting of her hair in chapter 7, Lucinda pulls out her doll's hair in clumps, turning the frivolous, ornamental doll into a sticky mess in a bid to replace her blonde hair with black locks. In so doing, Lucinda inadvertently transforms the doll's appearance so that she takes on some of the characteristics of an indigenous Australian, as Carey turns her act of vandalism into an extended conceit for what he himself is doing to the Victorian novel.

Elizabeth Gaskell and Thomas Hardy have also, thus far, received scant attention from revisionists, although as I shall discuss below, David Lodge's *Nice Work* sets up an exchange between 1980s Britain and the world of *North and South*. In Gaskell's case it is likely that literary revisionists have ignored her because she has only, comparatively recently, begun to receive the scholarly attention her work deserves. There have, however, been a number of popular television serializations of her work, including the BBC's highly successful *North and South* (2004), with its vivid scenes of snow-like cotton raining down on factory workers, and the later *Cranford* (2007).

Thomas Hardy has long been an important figure for the tourist industry in Dorset and the other areas that comprise Hardy's Wessex. The brewers Eldridge Pope manufactured a 'Thomas Hardy Ale' from 1968 until the brewery closed in 2003, with the bottles bearing Hardy's image. A Dorchester public house, 'The Trumpet Major', is named after one of Hardy's novels, while aficionados can undertake any number of tours featuring buildings and scenery which appeared in the novels, and even some of Hardy's previous homes.

Hardy's popularity is unquestionable, although it is not on the same scale as that of Dickens. It is therefore slightly perplexing that his work has not undergone the same type of reinvention and revision as Dickens' or Stoker's writing. Emma Tennant's *Tess* (1994) and Patricia Dolling-Mann's sequel to *Far From the Madding Crowd*, *Weatherbury Farm* (2008), are among the few examples of literary adaptations of Hardy's writing. Moreover, as Pamela Dalziel notes, although there were a small number of film and television productions of Thomas Hardy's novels in the twentieth century (including some silent films which appeared before his death in 1928 for which he negotiated rights), the novels were pretty much neglected by film-makers until the middle of the 1990s (Dalziel, 2007: 744). John Schlesinger's *Far from the Madding Crowd* (1967) and Roman Polanski's *Tess* (1979) were both highly popular, but at first glance it seems surprising that there were not more attempts to bring Hardy to the screen. According to Roy Pierce-Jones, Hardy was largely kept from television and radio schedules until the 1960s for moral reasons. Pierce-Jones comments of the BBC's practice of screening adaptations of 'classic' novels for a Sunday teatime family audience, 'Whilst Dickens's *Oliver Twist* could be softened and made more palatable for these audiences, Hardy's work could not' (Pierce-Jones, 2005: 65). It was only, he argues, the advent of the 1960s and the more relaxed attitudes towards representations of sex, class tensions and other previously taboo subjects which appear in Hardy's work that enabled Hardy to join the ranks of Dickens and the Brontës as fodder for classic serials or films. Curiously, it was Hardy's short stories that caught the interest of film-makers in the 1960s and it is only in more recent years that films including *The Return of the Native* (1994), *Jude* (1996) and *Under the Greenwood Tree* (2005) have appeared. *The Mayor of Casterbridge* has been adapted for film and television three times, in 1921 (a silent version), 1978 (by the playwright Dennis Potter) and 2001 (directed by David Thacker), and it has also been serialized by BBC Radio 4. The novel was transformed into an opera in 1951 by the composer Peter Tranchall, while it also experienced a rather unexpected afterlife through Michael Winterbottom's movie, *The Claim* (2000), which relocates the action to the gold fields of the American Wild West.

The vampire's afterlives

At the risk of sounding speculative, I would argue that few texts have been subject to the level of reinvention and reconfiguration accorded to Bram Stoker's *Dracula*. Fittingly enough for an undead vampire, *Dracula* has given rise to an entire industry and enjoys a rich and plentiful afterlife. Stoker's work itself harks back to earlier vampire stories, including John Polidori's *The Vampyre* (1819) and Sheridan Le Fanu's *Carmilla* (1872). However, it is almost impossible to quantify the number of novels, plays, movies and cultural artefacts that pay tribute to *Dracula*. In *Our Vampires, Ourselves* (1995), Nina Auerbach examines 'the Draculas who stalk and shape-shift through the twentieth century, adapting to changing romantic ideals' (1982: 101). She scrutinizes a range of vampire narratives from the nineteenth and twentieth centuries, charting how they have mutated through time, and, in the final chapter, she explores how tales of blood-drinkers shifted in the face on an apparent HIV epidemic in the 1980s (175). Through an analysis of texts including Brian Aldiss' novel *Dracula Unbound* (1991), Auerbach draws parallels between nineteenth-century fears surrounding syphilis – including Stoker's own – and more contemporary health issues. As Aldiss expresses it, Stoker's novel 'had alerted people to the dangers of vampirism. At the same time, it contained Stoker's encoded message of personal sorrow, as he fell sick of the disease that had ravaged mankind for centuries' (175). For Auerbach, Stoker's novel is a 'compendium of emergent phobias' (175) and it is perhaps for this reason that it continues to carry such a widespread appeal. Anne Rice's enormously popular 'Vampire Chronicles' have been bestsellers since the publication of the first book in the series, *Interview with the Vampire*, in 1976. Rice wrote this novel in response to her young daughter's death from leukaemia, and she has spoken in a number of interviews about the connection between her child's disease of the blood and her decision to write about blood-drinkers with eternal lives.

Popular culture is saturated with lighter adaptations of the *Dracula* story. In Melbourne and on the Gold Coast, visitors to

Australia flock to Dracula's dinner theatre, which claims to have 'wined, dined and horrified over 3,000,000 guests from all over the world'. Stage adaptations of the *Dracula* story include *The Dracula Spectacular, or Fangs Ain't What They Used To Be* by John Gardiner and Andrew Parr, which was performed throughout the 1980s, and Frank Wildhorn's *Dracula, the Musical*. There have also been several *Dracula* operas, including one staged in Colombia by the composer Héctor Fabio Torres Cardona (2005) and another performed at the Lancaster Opera House in 2005, written by Paul Ziemba. Francis Ford Coppola's *Bram Stoker's Dracula* (1992) won three Academy Awards and was highly popular with audiences on its release, although it is a single representative of a long line of film and television versions of Stoker's novel, stemming back to the unauthorized silent movie, *Nosferatu*, which was made in 1921. In everyday life, small children learn about numbers from the *Sesame Street*'s popular Count, while since 1971 American consumers have been able to eat the Count Chocula cereal at breakfast time. The recently popular *Buffy the Vampire Slayer* and *Twilight* series also owe enormous debts to *Dracula* and draw upon the master text for a number of vampirical characteristics. These are just a handful of examples of the extent to which Stoker's vampire has permeated our daily lives and the extraordinary influence that he continues to have on culture, high and low.

Influential reworkings

Ronald Thomas has remarked that '"the movies" have become the principal medium through which the Victorian novel, and even Victorian culture, has maintained its ghostly afterlife in modern society' (2000: 305). Thomas is right to suggest that for many, the experience of the Victorians is mediated through film or television. However, his comments downplay the significant public and academic interest in Neo-Victorian writing. As you might imagine, it is impossible to account for every Neo-Victorian novel, but some have undoubtedly been more influential than others. John Fowles' *The French Lieutenant's Woman* (1969), a novel that plays with the Victorian archetype of the 'fallen' or 'ruined' woman, remains enormously popular, as does the film adaptation starring Jeremy Irons (1981). Fowles' novel appears to be the story of a woman, Sarah Woodruff, who has been seduced and the obsession she sparks in the rather dull male protagonist Charles Smithson. Charles later learns, through a dramatic and somewhat brutal sexual encounter, that Sarah is a virgin and Fowles then offers his readers three alternative endings from which to choose, thus circumventing the realist novel's need for definitive closure.

Since the success of Fowles' work, Neo-Victorianism has become much more widespread. Novels like Michel Faber's *The Crimson Petal and the White* (2003) and Sarah Waters' *Tipping the Velvet* (1998) have attracted a very large readership and have drawn readers back to the nineteenth century. Today, there are so many Neo-Victorian novels in circulation that there is a scholarly journal devoted to them, and Neo-Victorian studies is establishing itself as a separate scholarly field. Nevertheless, there remains an important dialogue between the Victorian novel and its contemporary imitators and I would argue that it is still essential to consider works from both periods alongside one another. The Neo-Victorian novel often assumes a reader who is familiar with the nineteenth-century original he or she is pastiching, and it can be difficult for readers without knowledge of the original text to follow the jokes and references in a revision.

If we accept Andrea Kirchknopf's assertion that rewrites of Victorian novels 'keep the average length and structure' of their originals (2008: 54), then Charles Palliser's *The Quincunx* (1989) is the exemplar of the form. Palliser's mystery story is Dickensian in length (it is almost 1,200 pages), structure and style, although it is also influenced by the sensational mysteries of Dickens' friend and collaborator Wilkie Collins. Meticulously researched and wonderfully atmospheric, the novel features the classic Victorian orphan-hero, but depicts him and his struggles without the excessive sentiment that often characterizes Dickens' work. Commenting on the novel's labyrinthine plot structure and stylistic similarity to Dickens' writing, J. Hillis Miller asks us to consider how we would know whether we are reading an authentic Victorian novel or a counterfeit. He answers his own question by drawing our attention to 'a certain hyperbole or evident artifice in the imitated features [that] calls attention to them' (2004: 141) and while Palliser's prose superbly echoes Dickens', he refuses to make concessions to Victorian propriety or the Victorian reader's desire for a happy ending. Writing in an 'afterword', Palliser describes his work as an 'ironic reconstruction' (1212), pointing to an awareness of his novel's distinction from its Victorian original.

Michael Cox's two novels *The Meaning of Night: A Confession* (2006) and *The Glass of Time* (2008) brilliantly demonstrate the Neo-Victorian novel's intertextuality. Originally to have been part of a trilogy, Cox's death prevented the final book from being written. The two completed works are riveting mystery stories that are clearly influenced by the work of Charles Dickens, but also of sensation novelists including Mary Elizabeth Braddon and Wilkie Collins. Both plots revolve around deception, obsessive love and stolen identities and include clever references to more recent pastiches including Michael Cunningham's *The Hours* (1998), Peter Carey's *Jack Maggs* and Charles Palliser's *The Quincunx*, as a way of referencing their postmodern playfulness (for a detailed account of Cox's novels see Moore, 2011). Furthermore, both works are framed by prefaces from an imaginary editor, 'Professor J. J. Antrobus', whose job title, 'Professor of Post-Authentic Victorian Fiction' (Cox, 2006: 3) skilfully leads the reader to ask questions about what it means for a text to be 'real'.

David Lodge presents a superb pastiche of the Victorian novel in his highly popular *Nice Work* (1988). Set in the city of Rummidge, which closely resembles 1980s Birmingham, Lodge's novel is a brilliant collage of well-known nineteenth-century industrial novels. The central protagonist Dr. Robyn Penrose is a temporary lecturer in Victorian studies, who is required to participate in a 'shadow' scheme with the managing director of a local factory. As a left-wing feminist, she is horrified by the politics of the Managing Director, Vic Wilcox and the working conditions endured by the staff. Since her area of expertise is the nineteenth-century industrial novel, Robyn's experiences are interlaced with her lectures on texts by Charlotte Brontë, Charles Dickens, Elizabeth Gaskell and Charles Kingsley, which illuminate the challenges she faces in the factory. While Robyn cannot always see parallels between her own life and the novels she teaches and analyses, Lodge's omniscient narrator often draws out ironical connections for the reader's benefit. There are scenes which mimic well-known passages of Victorian novels, such as when Robyn (who has been teaching Gaskell's *North and South*) stands beside Vic as he addresses his workers, but instead of defending Vic against missiles as Margaret Hale does, Robyn dispatches a singing, stripping messenger hired to humiliate the managing director and who is, by coincidence, one of Robyn's students. If you have never read a Neo-Victorian novel before, *Nice Work* provides an excellent introduction, moving as it does between informative lectures about the Victorians and more modern scenes that imitate nineteenth-century fiction.

A. S. Byatt's *Possession* is, like *Nice Work*, a 'research novel', which shows academic characters in the present attempting to solve a puzzle from the past. Whereas Lodge's protagonist quotes from well-known Victorian novelists in her lectures and conversations, Byatt's novel incorporates some beautiful pastiches of Victorian poetry, some of which have been influenced by the work of Christina Rossetti. Byatt's novel is particularly concerned with history and memory and, writing from a feminist perspective, she asks important questions about how women were represented in literary history and signals how those without voices were sometimes able to leave clues or traces for posterity. Byatt takes the opportunity to lampoon recent trends in critical theory through a series of less-than-scrupulous academic characters, who have moved away from primary textual scholarship into a more disembodied mode of thinking. The two present-day central characters, Maud and Roland, are drawn into a story of secret love and betrayal as they learn about an illicit relationship between the poets Randolph Henry Ash and Christabel LaMotte. As they learn to read and interpret undiscovered poems and letters from the nineteenth century, Maud and Roland gradually learn to appreciate the value of a historicized approach to literature, gently assimilating a feminist approach into their understanding of the past. As Yu-ting Huang has noted, the 'memory work' Maud and Roland perform also requires a degree of intuition in approaching their subjects:

> Memory work helps Roland and Maud to reach another level of understanding that is not confined to linguistic and literary-theoretical analysis. Rather, the past – combining their feelings, imagination and emotion – becomes part of their lives and experience. (Huang, 2010)

On one level the 'possession' of the title signals owning the subject under research by knowing her or him inside out (indeed, Roland actually steals an undiscovered letter from the British Library, so great is his desire to 'possess' Ash), but on another, it signifies a type of supernatural experience or haunting, whereby the Victorian authors almost seem to possess the souls of the two modern-day researchers.

Not all adaptations are serious and scholarly. Steampunk novels blend speculative fiction with Victorianism, often with comic effects, as in Paul di Filippo's *Victoria* (1995) in which the queen is replaced by a clone. Dickens' *Oliver Twist* has been turned into a graphic novel by Penko Gelev and John Malam (2006, this version is aimed at school children), as well as by Hilary Burningham and Chris Rowlatt (2011). Self-proclaimed 'superauthor' Sherri Browning Erwin has penned the highly irreverent *Jane Slayre* (2010), which seeks to build on the popularity of Seth Grahame-Smith's brilliantly absurd *Pride and Prejudice and Zombies* (2009). Mixing Charlotte Brontë's prose with her own interest in the paranormal, Erwin sabotages this high Victorian text by populating it with vampires and werewolves and reimagining Jane as a demon slayer. It addition to slaying a variety of the novel's characters, Erwin also wilfully butchers some of the original novel's best-loved quotes, revising the (in)famous 'Reader, I married him' with which Jane begins her concluding chapter to the significantly less romantic 'Reader, I buried him' (Erwin, 2009: 386). While some of them are gently mocking and others downright disrespectful, the fact that the Victorian novel continues to excite so much interest and such a proliferation of reworkings is a testament to its continued influence across the globe.

Hauntings

In recent years Neo-Victorian scholars have been increasingly interested in why we are drawn to the Victorians. Possibly responding to Byatt's haunting trope in *Possession*, Katherine J. Renk has written of the 'colonial past that continues to haunt the present' (1999: 99) as one way to account for the growing number of Neo-Victorian works written from a postcolonial or decolonized perspective. Rosario Arias and Patricia Pulham have developed this idea of the novel as possessing a ghostly afterlife beyond its pages in a recent collection of essays that explore how Neo-Victorian novelists are 'haunted' by voices from the past. One contributor, Mark Llewellyn, cleverly inverts the idea of today's readers looking back to the past by arguing that the Victorians were just as invested in looking forward to their future and our present (in Arias and Pulham, 2010: 42). Furthermore, he reads Neo-Victorian writing as a type of séance, commenting, 'Through pastiche and revisioning, through the mesmeric nature of rereading, the ghostwriters of the present are playing an ambiguous game with a contemporary readership hungry for the summoned spirit of a Victorian fiction they believe in' (42). If the Neo-Victorian novel is a medium through which we can speak to the Victorians and they can talk back to us, then readers and writers put themselves in the position of Emily Brontë's Heathcliff, recklessly demanding to be haunted.

Llewellyn's ghostly motif is compellingly vivid, in that it almost goes so far as to suggest that should we overstep in our revisionism, then the Victorians will intervene to set us straight. Perhaps embedded within it, too, is a warning against trying too hard to erase the less palatable aspects of Victorian culture and to impose our own artistic and political agendas on the period. Regardless of whether we expect them to haunt us or not, it is clear that the Victorians are here to stay. As we look back on their past, we are able to learn more about the formation of the present, at the same time gasping with amazement at the energy, creativity and resourcefulness of this exhilarating time of change.

Reading

Neo-Victorianism

- Rosario Arias and Patricia Pulham (eds), *Haunting and Spectrality in Neo-Victorian Fiction: Possessing the Past* (2010)
- Jay Clayton, *Charles Dickens in Cyberspace: The Afterlife of the Nineteenth Century in Postmodern Culture* (2003)
- Ann Heilmann and Mark Llewellyn, *Neo-Victorianism: The Victorians in the Twenty-First Century, 1999–2009* (2010)
- Alice Jenkins and Juliet John (eds), *Rereading Victorian Fiction* (2000)
- Simon Joyce, *The Victorians in the Rearview Mirror* (2007)

Research

- What are the characteristics of a Neo-Victorian text? Using the 'rules' that Miriam Burstein lists on her 'Little Professor' blog as a starting point, try to identify some of the other conventions that shape revisions of the nineteenth-century novels. http://littleprofessor.typepad.com/the_little_professor /2006/03/rules_for_writi.html
- Consider how the Neo-Victorian novel engages with politics and/or official history.
- Think about the relationship between at least two Neo-Victorian novels and their 'parent' texts. Are the more recent texts antagonistic towards their predecessors, or is the relationship more reverential?
- Discuss why the novels of Charles Dickens and/or Charlotte Brontë are so popular with revisionist writers.
- Consider why contemporary writers are so drawn to the nineteenth century.
- How and why are some Neo-Victorian writers cavalier with historical facts?

Select webography

- Remember to approach electronic resources with caution. Anyone can post to the internet, so try to restrict yourself to legitimate scholarly sites, usually those hosted by institutions committed to scholarship like libraries, universities or museums.
- Use your internet research to supplement more traditional media like books and journal articles. Avoid using the internet as your only resource.
- Patrick Leary, who moderates the VICTORIA-L list, has produced a comprehensive survey of electronic research skills. See Patrick Leary (2004), 'Victorian Studies in the Digital Age', in Taylor and Wolff (eds), *The Victorians*

Since 1901, 201–14. Leary's essay 'Googling the Victorians' is also extremely useful for anyone beginning electronic research.

Dickens in Context: An extremely useful research tool put together by the British Library, incorporating contextual information about Dickens' life and times. www.bl.uk/learning/langlit/dickens/dickenshome.html

Dickens Journals Online: Led by John Drew, this scheme is gradually making every edition of Dickens' journals *Household Words* and *All the Year Round* available to readers. www.buckingham.ac.uk/djo

DICKENS-L: A helpful discussion list for Dickens scholars, students and enthusiasts, moderated by Professor Emeritus Patrick McCarthy of University of California, Santa Barbara. To subscribe to the list, email listserv@listserv.ucsb.edu and type the following message: SUB DICKNS-L YOURFIRSTNAME YOURLASTNAME

The Dickens Project: Based at University of California, Santa Cruz, the Dickens Project is an international consortium of scholars interested in nineteenth-century studies. The pages provide helpful links, articles and resources for teaching and research. http://dickens.ucsc.edu/

Discovering Dickens: Part of the Stanford Community Reading Project, these pages offer valuable contextual information, along with the experience of reading Dickens in parts. http://dickens.stanford.edu/dickens/

The Imperial Archive: Leon Litvack's Imperial Archive provides resources for those interested in nineteenth-century British imperialism, offering both historical contextual material and literary analyses. The site also includes a number of e-texts, including the controversial short story by Charles Dickens and Wilkie Collins, 'The Perils of Certain English Prisoners.' www.qub.ac.uk/schools/SchoolofEnglish/imperial/imperial.htm

The Literary Encyclopedia: A very helpful starting point for contextual material, containing short summaries of authors and their works by leading scholars in the field. www.litencyc.com/

Mitsuharu Matsuoka's pages: Professor Mitsuharu Matsuoka of Nagoya University, Japan, includes concordances, links and searchable e-texts relating to the Brontës, Dickens and Gaskell, among others. www.lang.nagoya-u.ac.jp/~matsuoka/

Monuments and Dust: This site is dedicated to the culture of Victorian London. Although it has not been updated in a while, this site includes an archive of materials relating to every aspect of Victorian life, from the suburban to the scandalous. www2.iath.virginia.edu/london/

Mousehold Words: While its name is a humorous tribute to Dickens' journal *Household Words*, this site uses technology to recapture the Victorian experience of reading in instalments. Readers can subscribe to the service without charge and will receive chapters according to their chosen reading schedule. http://mousehold-words.com/

Neo-Victorian Studies: A free public access journal edited by Mary-Luise Kohlke at the Centre for Neo-Victorian Studies, University of Swansea, Wales. The journal includes reviews and articles covering all aspects of revising the nineteenth century and will soon incorporate a database of Neo-Victorian resources. www.neovictorianstudies.com/

Nineteenth-Century Studies Online (NINES): NINES is a superbly ambitious site run at the University of Virginia. It includes blogs, exhibits, links to journals, publishers, e-texts and sites of interest, including the stunning Rossetti archive (www.rossettiarchive.org). The University of Virginia has always been at the forefront of using technology to bring the Victorians to life for twenty-first century readers and scholars, and this site is likely to develop in fascinating ways. www.nines.org/

The Little Professor: Miriam Elizabeth Burstein's blog includes a set of rules on how to write a Neo-Victorian novel and a superb collection of links to other Victorian research tools. Burstein discusses teaching and researching in Victorian literature and culture. http://littleprofessor.typepad.com

The Victoria Archives: Patrick Leary's VICTORIA-L list server is a wonderful resource for anyone interested in the Victorians. Scholars, students and enthusiasts all belong to the list and share their knowledge with anyone who has a query about life in the nineteenth century. You can search the archives using keywords to avoid duplicating a query and to draw on more than a decade of expertise. https://listserv.indiana.edu/cgi-bin/wa-iub.exe?A0=VICTORIA

The Victoria Web: George Landow's site is filled with useful information and links relating to Victorian literature and culture, and includes material on individual authors, bibliographies, reading lists and pages devoted to themes like gender, politics and class. www.victorianweb.org/

The Victorian Women Writers Project: This site aims to make nineteenth-century women's writing freely available to all readers. It will ultimately include anthologies, novels, political pamphlets, religious tracts, children's books and volumes of poetry and verse dramas. www.indiana.edu/~letrs/vwwp/

The Workhouse: With pictures, historical commentary and reminiscences from former inmates, the site provides a wonderful introduction to the often ghastly world of Parish Relief. www.workhouses.org.uk/

BIBLIOGRAPHY

Please also see the 'Reading' and 'Research' sections at the end of each chapter of this book.

Primary texts (Victorian)

Brontë, Charlotte. *Jane Eyre*. 1847. Ed. Richard J. Dunn. New York, NY: W.W. Norton, 1987.

Carlyle, Thomas. *Shooting Niagara*. London: Chapman & Hall, 1867.

—. *Chartism* in *Thomas Carlyle: Selected Writings*. Ed. Alan Shelston. Harmondsworth, Middlesex: Penguin, 1980.

Cobbe, Frances Power. 'What Shall We Do with Our Old Maids?' in Susan Hamilton (ed.), *Criminals, Idiots, Women & Minors: Victorian Writing by Women on Women*. Peterborough, Ontario: Broadview, 1994, 59.

Dickens, Charles. *Oliver Twist*. 1837. Oxford: Oxford University Press, The Oxford Illustrated Dickens, 1994.

—. *The Letters of Charles Dickens, volume 7, 1853–1855*. Ed. Graham Storey, Kathleen Tillotson, Angus Easson. (Pilgrim Edition). Oxford: Clarendon Press, 1993.

Disraeli, Benjamin. *Sybil, or the Two Nations*. 1845. Ed. Sheila M. Smith. Oxford: Oxford University Press, 1981.

Eliot, George. *Adam Bede*. 1859. Ed. Stephen Gill. Harmondsworth, Middlesex: Penguin, 1980.

—. *The Mill on the Floss*. 1860. Ed. A. S. Byatt. Harmondsworth, Middlesex: Penguin, 1985.

—. 'Silly Novels by Lady Novelists' in *The Essays of 'George Eliot'*. Middlesex: Echo, 2009, 124–41.

Gaskell, Elizabeth. *North and South*. 1854–5. Ed. Angus Easson. Oxford: Oxford University Press, 1998.

Hardy, Thomas. *The Mayor of Casterbridge*. 1886. Ed. Dale Kramer. Oxford: Oxford University Press, 1990.

—. *Jude the Obscure*. 1895. Ed. Patricia Ingham. Oxford: Oxford University Press, 1989.

Mayhew, Henry. *London Labour and the London Poor in Four Volumes*. 1851–62. Dover Publications, 1983.
Newman, John Henry. *The Idea of a University*. 1852. Ed. Frank M. Turner. New Haven, CT and London: Yale University Press, 1996.
Ruskin, John. *Sesame and Lilies*. Ed. Deborah Epstein Nord. New Haven, CT: Yale University Press, 2002.
Seeley, John R. *The Expansion of England: Two Courses of Lectures*. London: Macmillan, 1907.
Stoker, Bram. *Dracula*. 1897. Ed. Maud Ellmann. Oxford: Oxford University Press, 1996.

Primary texts (Neo-Victorian)

Byatt, A. S. *Possession: A Romance*. 1990. London: Vintage, 1991.
Carey, Peter. *Oscar and Lucinda*. 1988. London and Boston: Faber & Faber, 1989.
Condé, Maryse. *Windward Heights*. 1998. New York: Soho Press, 2000.
Cox, Michael. *The Meaning of Night*. 2006. London: John Murray, 2007.
—. *The Glass of Time*. London: John Murray, 2008.
Di Filippo, Paul. *The Steampunk Trilogy*. 1995. New York: Four Walls Eight Windows, 1997.
Erwin, Sherri Browning. *Jane Slayre: The Literary Classic with a Blood-Sucking Twist*. New York: Gallery Books, 2010.
Flanagan, Richard. *Wanting*. Sydney: Knopf, 2008.
Gelev, Penko and John Malam. *Oliver Twist*. New York: Barron's Educational Series, 2006.
Jones, Lloyd. *Mister Pip*. 2006. London: John Murray, 2007.
Lodge, David. *Nice Work*. 1988. Harmondsworth, Middlesex: Penguin, 1990.
Palliser, Charles. *The Quincunx*. 1989. Harmondsworth, Middlesex: Penguin, 1990.
Rhys, Jean. *Wide Sargasso Sea*. 1966. Harmondsworth, Middlesex: Penguin, 1968.
Simmons, Dan. *Drood: A Novel*. London: Quercus, 2009.
Woolf, Virginia. *Orlando: A Biography*. 1928. London: Harcourt, 1956.
—. 'Professions for Women' in *The Death of the Moth and Other Essays*. London: Hogarth Press, 1947.
—. 'Mr. Bennett and Mrs. Brown.' 1924, in *Virginia Woolf: Selected Essays*. Ed. David Bradshaw. Oxford: Oxford University Press, 2008, 32–6.

Secondary sources

Altick, Richard D. *Victorian People and Ideas: A Companion for the Modern Reader of Victorian Literature*. New York: W.W. Norton, 1973.

Arata, Stephen D. 'The Occidental Tourist: Dracula and the Anxiety of Reverse Colonization'. *Victorian Studies*, 33, 4, Summer 1990, 621–45.

—. *Fictions of Loss at the Fin de Siècle: Identity and Empire*. Cambridge: Cambridge University Press, 2009.

Archibald, Diana. *Domesticity, Imperialism and Emigration in the Victorian Novel*. Columbia: University of Missouri Press, 2002.

Arias, Rosario and Patricia Pulham (eds). *Haunting and Spectrality in Neo-Victorian Fiction: Possessing the Past*. Houndmills: Palgrave Macmillan, 2010.

Armstrong, Nancy. *Desire and Domestic Fiction: A Political History of the Novel*. Oxford: Oxford University Press, 1987.

Auerbach, Nina. *Woman and the Demon: the Life of a Victorian Myth*. Cambridge, MA: Harvard University Press, 1982.

—. *Our Vampires, Ourselves*. Chicago and London: University of Chicago Press, 1995.

Beer, Gillian. *Darwin's Plots: Evolutionary Narratives in Darwin, George Eliot and Nineteenth-Century Fiction* 1983 (3rd edn). Cambridge: Cambridge University Press, 2009.

Bennett, Andrew and Nicholas Royle. *An Introduction to Literature, Criticism and Theory* (2nd edn). New York: Prentice Hall, 1999.

Birch, Dinah. *Our Victorian Education*. Oxford: Blackwell, 2008.

Bloom, Harold (ed.). *The Victorian Novel*. New York: Chelsea House Publications, 2004.

Boehmer, Elleke. *Colonial and Postcolonial Literature: Migrant Metaphors*. Oxford: Oxford University Press, 1995.

Botting, Fred. *Gothic*. London: Routledge, 1996.

Bourke, Joanna. *Fear: A Cultural History*. London: Virago, 2005.

Brantlinger, Patrick. *Rule of Darkness: British Literature and Imperialism, 1830–1914*. Ithaca, NY: Cornell University Press, 1990.

—. *Fictions of State: Culture and Credit in Britain, 1694–1994*. Ithaca, NY: Cornell University Press, 1996.

Briggs, Asa. *Victorian Cities*. 1963. Harmondsworth, Middlesex: Penguin, 1990.

—. *Chartism*. Stroud: Sutton Publishing, 1998.

Bristow, Joseph. 'Why Victorian? A Period and its Problems'. *Literature Compass*, 1, February 2004, 1–16.

Brooks, Chris. *Signs for the Times: Symbolic Realism in the Mid-Victorian World*. London: George Allen & Unwin, 1984.

Clayton, Jay. *Charles Dickens in Cyberspace: The Afterlife of the Nineteenth Century in Postmodern Culture.* New York: Oxford University Press, 2003.

Collins, Philip. *Dickens and Education.* London: Macmillan, 1964.

Corbett, Mary Jean. '"The Crossing o' Breeds" in *The Mill on the Floss*' in Deborah Denenholz Morse and Martin A. Danahay (eds), *Victorian Animal Dreams: Representations of Animals in Victorian Literature and Culture.* Aldershot and Burlington, VT: Ashgate, 2007, 121–44.

—. *Family Likeness: Sex, Marriage and Incest from Jane Austen to Virginia Woolf.* Ithaca, NY: Cornell University Press, 2008.

Corpron Parker, Pamela. 'Fictional Philanthropy in Elizabeth Gaskell's *Mary Barton* and *North and South*'. *Victorian Literature and Culture,* 25, 1997, 321–31.

Craft, Christopher. 'Kiss Me with Those Red Lips: Gender and Inversion in Bram Stoker's *Dracula*'. *Representations*, 8, Autumn 1984. 107–33.

Dalziel, Pamela. 'Thomas Hardy on Screen, and: Seeing Hardy: Film and Television Adaptations of the Fiction of Thomas Hardy'. *Victorian Studies*, 49, 4, Summer 2007, 744–6.

Danahay, Martin. *Gender at Work in Victorian Culture, Literature, Arts and Masculinity.* Aldershot and Burlington, VT: Ashgate, 2005.

David, Deirdre. *Fictions of Resolution in Three Victorian Novels: North and South, Our Mutual Friend, Daniel Deronda.* London: Macmillan, 1981.

Davidoff, Leonore and Catherine Hall. *Family Fortunes: Men and Women of the English Middle Class 1780–1850.* Chicago, IL: University of Chicago Press, 1987.

Davis, Lance E. and Robert A. Huttenback. *Mammon and the Pursuit of Empire: The Political Economy of British Imperialism, 1860–1912.* New York: Cambridge University Press, 1986.

Davis, Philip. *The Oxford English Literary History, Volume 8, 1830–1880: The Victorians.* 2002. Oxford: Oxford University Press, 2004.

Dennis, Barbara. *The Victorian Novel* (Cambridge Contexts in Literature). Cambridge: Cambridge University Press, 2000.

Dowling, Linda. 'The Decadent and the New Woman in the 1890s' in Lyn Pykett (ed.), *Reading Fin de Siècle Fictions.* London and New York: Longman, 1996, 47–63.

Eagleton, Terry. *Marxism and Literary Criticism.* Berkeley: University of California Press, 1976.

—. *The English Novel: An Introduction.* Oxford: Blackwell, 2005.

—. *Myths of Power: A Marxist Study of the Brontës.* 1975 (Anniversary Edition). Houndmills: Palgrave Macmillan, 2005

Eliot, Simon. 'The Business of Victorian Publishing' in Deirdre David (ed.), *The Cambridge Companion to the Victorian Novel.* Cambridge: Cambridge University Press, 2001, 37–60.

Ellis, Steve. *Virginia Woolf and the Victorians*. Cambridge: Cambridge University Press, 2007.

Engels, Friedrich. 'The Great Towns' in Richard T. Le Gates and Frederic Stout (eds), *The City Reader* (2nd edn). London and New York: Routledge, 2001, 46–55.

Flint, Kate. 'George Eliot and Gender' in George L. Levine (ed.), *The Cambridge Companion to George Eliot*. Cambridge: Cambridge University Press, 2001, 159–80.

—. 'Why "Victorian"? Response'. *Victorian Studies*, 47, 2, Winter 2005, 230–9.

Flynn, Suzanne J. 'Hardy in (a time of) Transition' in Rosemarie Morgan (ed.), *The Ashgate Research Companion to Thomas Hardy*. Burlington VT and Farnham, Surrey: Ashgate, 2010.

Foucault, Michel. *The History of Sexuality, Volume One: The Will to Knowledge*. 1976. Trans. Robert Hurley. Harmondsworth: Middlesex, Penguin 1990.

Fraser, Hilary. *Beauty and Belief: Aesthetics and Religion in Victorian Literature*. Cambridge: Cambridge University Press, 2008.

Freedgood, Elaine. *Factory Production in Nineteenth-Century Britain*. Oxford: Oxford University Press, 2003.

Freeman, Nicholas. *Conceiving the City: London, Literature and Art 1870–1914*. Oxford: Oxford University Press, 2007.

Furneaux, Holly. *Queer Dickens: Erotics, Families, Masculinities*. Oxford: Oxford University Press, 2010.

Gagnier, Regenia. *The Insatiability of Human Wants: Economics and Aesthetics in Market Society*. Chicago, IL: University of Chicago Press, 2000.

—. *Individualism, Decadence and Globalization: On the Relationship of Part to Whole, 1859–1920*. Basingstoke: Palgrave, 2010.

Gallagher, Catherine. *The Industrial Reformation of English Fiction: Social Discourse and Narrative Form, 1832–1867*. Chicago, IL: University of Chicago Press, 1985.

—. *The Body Economic: Life, Death and Sensation in Political Economy and the Victorian Novel*. Princeton, NJ: Princeton University Press, 2008.

Garrard, Greg. *Ecocriticism*. London and New York: Routledge, 2007.

Gay, Penny, Judith Johnston and Cathy Waters. *Victorian Turns, Neo-Victorian Returns: Essays on Fiction and Culture*. Cambridge: Cambridge Scholars Press, 2008.

Gilbert, Pamela K. *Cholera and Nation: Doctoring the Social Body in Victorian England*. Albany, NY: SUNY Press, 2008.

Gilbert, Sandra and Susan Gubar. *The Madwoman in the Attic: The Woman Writer and the Nineteenth-Century Literary Imagination*. 1979. New Haven, CT: Yale University Press, 2000.

Gilmour, Robin. *The Idea of the Gentleman in the Victorian Novel.* London: George Allen & Unwin, 1981.

—. *The Victorian Period: The Intellectual and Cultural Context of English Literature.* London: Longman, 1994.

Girard, René. *Deceit, Desire and the Novel: Self and Other in Literary Structure.* Trans. Yvonne Freccero. Baltimore and London: Johns Hopkins, 1965.

Goodlad, Lauren M. E. *Victorian Literature and the Victorian State: Character and Governance in a Liberal Society.* Baltimore: Johns Hopkins University Press, 2003.

Grey, Drew D. *London's Shadows: The Dark Side of the Victorian City.* London and New York: Continuum, 2010.

Gutleben, Christian. *Nostalgic Postmodernism: The Victorian Tradition and the Contemporary British Novel.* Amsterdam and New York: Rodopi, 2001.

Guy, Josephine M. *The Victorian Social-Problem Novel.* Houndmills: Palgrave Macmillan, 1996.

Hack, Daniel. *The Material Interests of the Victorian Novel.* Charlottesville: University of Virginia Press, 2005.

Hager, Kelly. *Dickens and the Rise of Divorce: The Failed-Marriage Plot and the Novel Tradition.* Burlington, VT and Farnham, Surrey: Ashgate, 2010.

Halberstam, Judith. 'Technologies of Monstrosity: Bram Stoker's *Dracula*' in Sally Ledger and Scott McCracken (eds), *Cultural Politics at the Fin de Siècle.* Cambridge: Cambridge University Press, 1995, 248–66.

Harman, Barbara Leah. *The Feminine Political Novel in Victorian England.* Charlottesville, VA: University of Virginia Press, 1998.

Hartley, Jenny. *Charles Dickens and the House of Fallen Women.* London: Methuen, 2008.

Heilmann, Ann and Mark Llewellyn. *Neo-Victorianism: The Victorians in the Twenty-First Century, 1999–2009.* Basingstoke: Palgrave, 2010.

Herbert, Christopher. 'Vampire Religion'. *Representations*, 79, Summer 2002, 100–21.

Himmelfarb, Gertrude. *The Idea of Poverty: England in the Early Industrial Age.* New York: Knopf, 1984.

Huang, Yu-ting. 'Burn What They Should Not See: Family Secrets in A. S. Byatt's *Possession*'. *Traffic,* 11, 2010. www.gsa.unimelb.edu.au/Traffic11/Traffic_11_contents.shtml

Hughes, Kathryn. *The Victorian Governess.* London and Ohio: Hambledon Press, 1993.

Ingham, Patricia. *The Language of Gender and Class: Transformation in the Victorian Novel.* London and New York: Routledge, 1996.

Jenkins, Alice and Juliet John (eds). *Rereading Victorian Fiction.* Houndmills: Palgrave Macmillan, 2000.

John, Juliet. *Dickens and Mass Culture*. Oxford: Oxford University Press, 2010.

Joyce, Simon. *Geographies of Class and Crime in Victorian London*. Charlottesville and London: University of Virginia Press, 2003.

—. *The Victorians in the Rearview Mirror*. Athens, OH: Ohio University Press, 2007.

Kaplan, Cora. *Victoriana: Histories, Fictions, Criticism*. Edinburgh: Edinburgh University Press, 2007.

Keating, Peter. *The Working Classes in Victorian Fiction*. London: Routledge & Kegan Paul, 1971.

Keen, Suzanne. *Romances of the Archive in Contemporary British Fiction*. London and Toronto: University of Toronto Press, 2001.

Kincaid, James R. *Child-Loving: The Erotic Child and Victorian Culture*. New York: Routledge, 1992.

Kirchknopf, Andrea. '(Re)workings of Nineteenth-Century Fiction'. *Neo-Victorian Studies*, 1, 1, Autumn 2008, 53–80.

Knight, Mark and Emma Mason. *Nineteenth-Century Religion and Literature: An Introduction*. Oxford: Oxford University Press, 2006.

Kohlke, Mary-Louise and Christian Gutleben (eds). *Neo-Victorian Tropes of Trauma: The Politics of Bearing After-Witness to Nineteenth-Century Suffering*. Amsterdam and NewYork: Rodopi, 2010.

Koven, Seth. *Sexual and Social Politics in Victorian London*. Princeton, NJ: Princeton University Press, 2004.

Krueger, Christine L. (ed.). *Functions of Victorian Culture at the Present Time*. Athens: Ohio University Press, 2002.

Kucich, John and Dianne Sadoff. *Victorian Afterlife: Postmodern Culture Rewrites the Nineteenth Century*. Minneapolis and London: University of Minnesota Press, 2000.

Lane, Lauriat Jr. 'Dickens's Archetypal Jew'. *PMLA*, 73, 1, March 1958, 94–100.

Leary, Patrick. 'Googling the Victorians'. *Journal of Victorian Culture*, 10, 1, Spring 2005, 72–86.

Ledger, Sally. *The New Woman: Fiction and Feminism at the Fin de Siècle*. Manchester: Manchester University Press, 1997.

—. *Dickens and the Popular Radical Imagination*. Cambridge: Cambridge University Press, 2007.

Levine, George. *Darwin and the Novelists: Patterns of Science in Victorian Fiction*. Cambridge, MA: Harvard University Press, 1988.

—. *How to Read the Victorian Novel*. Oxford: Blackwell, 2008.

Llewellyn, Mark. 'What is Neo-Victorian Studies?' *Neo-Victorian Studies*, 1, 1, Autumn 2008, 164–85.

Lonoff, Sue. 'Disseminating Victorian Culture' in Christine L. Krueger (ed.), *Functions of Victorian Culture at the Present Time*. Athens, OH: Ohio University Press, 2002, 171–82.

Mancoff, Debra N. and D. J. Trela (eds). *Victorian Urban Settings: Essays on the Nineteenth-Century City and its Contexts*. New York, NY: Garland, 2007.

Marcus, Sharon. *Between Women: Friendship, Desire and Marriage in Victorian England*. Princeton, NJ: Princeton University Press, 2007.

Marcus, Steven. *The Other Victorians: A Study of Sexuality and Pornography in Mid-Nineteenth-Century England*. 1966. New York, NY: Basic Books, 1975.

Marshall, Gail (ed.). *The Cambridge Companion to the Fin de Siècle*. Cambridge: Cambridge University Press, 2007.

Mason, Michael. *The Making of Victorian Sexuality*. Oxford: Oxford University Press, 1994.

Meyer, Susan. *Imperialism at Home: Race and Victorian Women's Fiction*. Ithaca, NY: Cornell University Press, 1996.

Miller, J. Hillis. 'Parody as Revisionary Critique: Charles Palliser's *The Quincunx*'. *Postmodern Studies*, 35, 2004, 129–48.

Mitchell, Kate. *Victorian Afterimages: History and Cultural Memory in Neo-Victorian Fiction*. Basingstoke: Palgrave, 2009.

Moore, Grace. 'Beastly Criminals and Criminal Beasts: Stray Women and Stray Dogs in *Oliver Twist*' in Deborah Denenholz Morse and Martin A. Danahay (eds), *Victorian Animal Dreams: Representations of Animals in Victorian Literature and Culture*. Aldershot and Burlington, VT: Ashgate, 2007, 201–14.

—. 'Twentieth-Century Re-Workings of the Victorian Novel'. *Literature Compass*, 5, 1, 2008, 134–44.

—. 'Neo-Victorian and Pastiche' in Pamela K. Gilbert (ed.), *A Companion to Sensation Fiction*. Oxford: Blackwell, 2011, 627–38.

Moregentaler, Goldie. *Dickens and Heredity: When Like Begets Like*. Basingstoke: Macmillan, 2000.

Moretti, Franco. *Signs Taken for Wonders: On the Sociology of Literary Forms*. 1983. London: Verso, 2005.

—. *The Way of the World: The Bildungsroman in European Culture*. Trans. Albert J. Sbragia. London: Verso, 1987.

Morgan, Rosemarie (ed.). *The Ashgate Research Companion to Thomas Hardy*. Burlington, VT and Farnham, Surrey: Ashgate, 2010.

Morris, Pam. *Realism*. 2003. Oxford: Routledge, 2009.

Morse, Deborah Denenholz. 'Mutiny on the Orion: The Legacy of the *Hermione* Mutiny and the Politics of nonviolent Protest in Elizabeth Gaskell's *North and South*' in Grace Moore (ed.) *Pirates and Mutineers of the Nineteenth Century: Swashbucklers and Swindlers*. Burlington, VT and Farnham, Surrey: Ashgate, 2011, 117–32.

Mosley, Stephen. *The Chimney of the World: A History of Smoke Pollution in Victorian and Edwardian Manchester*. 2001. London and New York: Routledge, 2008.

Nead, Lynda. *Victorian Babylon: People, Streets and Images in Nineteenth-Century London*. New Haven, CT: Yale University Press, 2000.

Newsom, Robert. 'Religion' in Paul Schlicke (ed.), *The Oxford Reader's Companion to Dickens*. Oxford: Oxford University Press, 1999, 490–4.

Nord, Deborah Epstein. *Walking the Victorian Streets: Women, Representation and the City*. Ithaca and London: Cornell University Press, 1995.

O'Gorman, Francis. 'Where Next in Victorian Studies?—Introduction'. *Literature Compass*, 4, June 2007, 1277–9.

—. (ed.). *Victorian Literature and Finance*. Oxford: Oxford University Press, 2007.

Oulton, Carolyn W. de la L. *Literature and Religion in Mid-Victorian England: From Dickens to Eliot*. Basingstoke: Palgrave, 2003.

Parsons, Deborah. *Streetwalking the Metropolis: Women, the City and Modernity*. Oxford: Oxford University Press, 2001.

Pearsall, Ronald. *The Worm in the Bud: The World of Victorian Sexuality*. 1969. Harmondsworth, Middlesex: Penguin, 1972.

Peters, Laura. *Orphan Texts: Victorian Orphans, Culture & Empire*. Manchester: Manchester University Press, 2001.

Pierce-Jones, Roy. 'Screening the Short Stories: From the 1950s to the 1990s' in T. R. Wright (ed.) *Thomas Hardy on Screen*. Cambridge: Cambridge University Press, 2005, 63–75.

Pite, Ralph. ' "His Country": Hardy in the Rural' in Keith Wilson (ed.), *A Companion to Thomas Hardy*. Oxford: Blackwell, 2009. 133–45.

Plotz, John. *The Crowd: British Literature and Public Politics*. Berkeley and Los Angeles: University of California Press, 2000.

—. *Portable Property: Victorian Culture on the Move*. Princeton, NJ: Princeton University Press, 2008.

Politi, Jina. '*Jane Eyre* classified'. *Literature and History*, 8, 1982, 56–66.

Poovey, Mary. *Uneven Developments: The Ideological Work of Gender in Mid-Victorian England*. 1988. London: Virago, 1989.

—. *Making a Social Body: British Cultural Formation 1830–1864*. Chicago, IL: University of Chicago Press, 1995.

—. *Genres of the Credit Economy: Mediating Value in Eighteenth and Nineteenth-Century Literature*. Chicago, IL: University of Chicago Press, 2008.

Pykett, Lyn. *Reading Fin de Siècle Fictions*. London: Longman, 1996.

Ragussis, Michael. *Figures of Conversion: The Jewish Question and English National Identity*. Durham, NC: Duke University Press, 1995.

Renk, Kathleen J. *Caribbean Shadows and Victorian Ghosts: Women's Writing and Decolonization*. Charlottesville, VA: University Press of Virginia, 1999.

Richards, Thomas. *The Imperial Archive: Knowledge and the Fantasy of Empire*. London and New York: Verso, 1996.
Richardson, Angelique. *Love and Eugenics in the Late Nineteenth Century*. Oxford: Oxford University Press, 2003.
Richardson, Angelique and Chris Willis. *The New Woman in Fiction and in Fact: Fin-de-Siècle Feminisms*. Houndmills: Palgrave Macmillan, 2000.
Said, Edward. *Orientalism: Western Conceptions of the Orient*. 1978. Harmondsworth, Middlesex: Penguin, 1995.
Samuel, Raphael. *Theatres of Memory: Volume I, Past and Present in Contemporary Culture*. 1994. London: Verso, 1996.
Schaffer, Talia. 'A Wilde Desire Took Me: The Homoerotic History of *Dracula*'. *ELH*, 61, 2, Summer 1994. 381–425.
—. '"Nothing but Foolscap and Ink": Inventing the New Woman' in Angelique Richardson and Chris Willis (eds), *The New Woman in Fiction and in Fact: Fin-de-Siècle Feminisms*. Houndmills: Basingstoke, 2001, 39–52.
Sedgwick, Eve Kosofsky. *Between Men: English Literature and Homosocial Desire*. New York, NY: Columbia University Press, 1985.
—. *Epistemology of the Closet*. 1990. Berkeley and Los Angeles: University of California Press, 2008.
Seltzer, Mark. 'Serial Killers (1)'. *Differences*, 5, 1, 1993, 92–129.
—. *Serial Killers: Death and Life in America's Wound Culture*. New York, NY: Routledge, 1998.
Sennett, Richard. *The Fall of Public Man: On the Social Psychology of Capitalism*. 1974. London: Vintage, 1976.
Sharpe, Jenny. *Allegories of Empire: The Figure of Woman in the Colonial Text*. Minneapolis and London: University of Minnesota Press, 1993.
Shattock, Joanne. 'Where Next in Victorian Literary Studies? – Revising the Canon, Extending Cultural Boundaries, and the Challenge of Interdisciplinarity'. *Literature Compass*, 4, June 2007, 1280–91.
Shiller, Dana. 'The Redemptive Past in the Neo-Victorian Novel'. *Studies in the Novel*, 29, 4, Winter 1997, 538–60.
Showalter, Elaine. *A Literature of Their Own: British Women Novelists from Brontë to Lessing*. 1979, (New revised edition). London: Virago, 1982.
—. 'The Unmanning of the Mayor of Casterbridge' in Dale Kramer (ed.), *Critical Approaches to the Fiction of Thomas Hardy*. London: Macmillan, 1979, 99–115.
—. *The Female Malady: Women, Madness and English Culture, 1830–1980*. 1985. London: Virago, 2007.
—. *Sexual Anarchy: Gender and Culture at the Fin de Siècle*. 1992. London: Virago, 1996.

Shuttleworth, Sally. *George Eliot and Nineteenth-Century Science: The Make-Believe of a Beginning*. Cambridge: Cambridge University Press, 1984.

Smith, Sheila M. *The Other Nation: The Poor in English Novels of the 1840s and 1850s*. Oxford: Clarendon Press, 1980.

Spivak, Gayatri. 'Three Women's Texts and a Critique of Imperialism'. *Critical Inquiry*, 12, 1; *Race, Writing and Difference*, Autumn 1985, 243–61.

Stone, Harry. 'Dickens and the Jews'. *Victorian Studies*, 2, 1959, 223–53.

Stoneman, Patsy. *Brontë Transformations: the Cultural Dissemination of Jane Eyre and Wuthering Heights*. London: Harvester Wheatsheaf, 1996.

Taylor, Miles and Michael Wolff (eds). *The Victorians Since 1901: Histories, Representations and Revisions*. Manchester: Manchester University Press, 2004.

Thieme, John. *Postcolonial Con-Texts: Writing Back to the Canon*. London: Continuum, 2001.

Thomas, Ronald R. 'Specters of the Novel: *Dracula* and the Cinematic Afterlife of the Victorian Novel' in Dianne F. Sadoff and John Kucich (eds), *Victorian Afterlife: Postmodern Culture Rewrites the Nineteenth Century*. Minneapolis and London: University of Minnesota Press, 2000, 288–310.

Thomas, Sue. *Imperialism, Reform and the Making of Englishness in Jane Eyre*. Basingstoke: Palgrave, 2008.

Tosh, John. *Manliness and Masculinities in Nineteenth-Century Britain*. London: Pearson, 2005.

Vicinus, Martha. *Suffer and be Still: Women in the Victorian Age*. Bloomington: Indiana University Press, 1972.

Wagner, Tamara S. *Financial Speculation in Victorian Fiction: Plotting, Money and the Novel Genre, 1851–1901*. Columbus, OH: Ohio State University Press, 2010.

Walkowitz, Judith. *City of Dreadful Delight: Narratives of Sexual Danger in Late-Victorian London*. 1992. London: Virago, 1998.

Waller, John. *The Real Oliver Twist: Robert Blincoe, a Life that Illuminates an Age*. Crows Nest, NSW: George Allen & Unwin, 2005.

Waters, Catherine. *Dickens and the Politics of the Family*. Cambridge: Cambridge University Press, 1997.

Watt, Ian. *The Rise of the Novel: Studies in Defoe, Richardson and Fielding*. 1957. Berkeley and Los Angeles, CA: University of California Press, 2001.

Weedon, Alexis. *Victorian Publishing: The Economics of Book Production for a Mass Market, 1836–1916*. Aldershot and Burlington, VT: Ashgate, 2003.

Weiss, Barbara. *The Hell of the English: Bankruptcy and the Victorian Novel*. Cranbury, NJ: Associated University Presses, 1986.

Williams, Raymond. *Culture and Society: Coleridge to Orwell*. 1958. London: Hogarth Press, 1982.

—. *The English Novel from Dickens to Lawrence*. London: Chatto & Windus, 1970.

—. *The Country and the City*. 1973. London: Hogarth Press, 1993.

Wisnicki, Adrian. *Conspiracy, Revolution and Terrorism from Victorian Fiction to the Modern Novel*. London and New York: Routledge, 2008.

Wohl, Anthony S. *The Victorian Family: Structures and Stresses*. New York, NY: St. Martins Press, 1978.

Wolff, Larry. '"The Boys are Pickpockets, and the Girl is a Prostitute": Gender and Juvenile Criminality in Early Victorian England from *Oliver Twist* to *London Labour*'. *NLH*, 27, 2, Spring 1996, 227–49.

Young, Arlene. *Culture, Class and Gender in the Victorian Novel: Gentlemen, Gents and Working Women*. Basingstoke: Macmillan, 1999.

Zanger, Jules. 'A Sympathetic Vibration: Dracula and the Jews'. *English Literature in Transition, 1880–1920*, 34, 1, 1991, 33–44.

Zieger, Susan. 'Dickens's Queer Children'. *LIT: Literature Interpretation Theory*, 20, 1–2, January–June 2009, 141–57.

INDEX

Aldiss, Brian,
Dracula Unbound 145
Allen, Grant,
The Woman Who Did 28, 72
Altick, Richard D. 11, 38
Amigoni, David 126
Arias, Rosario 150–1
Armstrong, Nancy 128
Arnold, Matthew 106, 120
Auerbach, Nina 81, 145
Austen, Jane 39
Mansfield Park 23

Baden-Powell, Robert 32
Balcombe, Florence 29
Bart, Lionel,
Oliver! 138
Bate, Jonathan 131
Beale, Dorothea 19
Beardsley, Aubrey 135
Beer, Gillian 5, 75, 107, 123–6, 133
Bentham, Jeremy 13
Betjeman, John (Sir) 137
Bildungsroman 2, 39–40, 77, 116
Birch, Dinah 67, 104
Blake, William,
Songs of Experience 31
Boehmer, Elleke 35, 132
Boer Wars (1880–1 and 1899–1902) 32, 36
Booth, William (General) 31
In Darkest England 32
Botting, Fred 89
Bourke, Joanna 12
Braddon, Mary Elizabeth 148
Briggs, Asa 14, 15
Bristow, Joseph 9
Brontë, Anne 115, 132
Brontë, Charlotte 35, 40, 114, 132, 148, 150, 152, 154
Jane Eyre 3, 42, 57–9, 69, 70–1, 77, 81–2, 97–9, 101–3, 113, 115, 117–20, 127, 133, 134, 139–40, 142, 143
Villette 115, 116
Brontë, Emily 114, 118, 132
Wuthering Heights 115, 139, 141, 142, 151
Brontë Parsonage Museum (Haworth, Yorkshire, UK) 138
Brooks, Chris 42
Buell, Lawrence 131
Buffy the Vampire Slayer 146
Burningham, Hilary 150
Burstein, Miriam Elizabeth (The Little Professor) 141–2, 152, 154
Buss, Mary 19
Butler, Judith 122
Butler, Samuel 135
Byatt, A.S.,
Possession 141, 149

Cameron, Julia Margaret 137
Cardona, Héctor Fabio Torres 146

Carey, Peter,
Jack Maggs 142, 148
Oscar and Lucinda 143
Carlyle, Thomas 11, 12, 16, 41, 124
Catholic Relief Act (1829) 21
Chambers, Robert,
Vestiges of the Natural History of Creation 23
Chartism 14–17
Chisholm, Caroline 34
Clayton, Jay 132, 151
Cobbe, Frances Power,
'What Shall We Do with Our Old Maids?' 27
Collins, Wilkie 123, 147, 148, 153
The Moonstone 35
Condé, Maryse,
Windward Heights 141
Coppola, Francis Ford,
Bram Stoker's Dracula 146
Corbett, Mary Jean 74, 108
Corn Laws 15, 90, 114
Cornhill, The 4
Coutts, Angela Burdett 79
Cox, Michael,
The Glass of Time 148
The Meaning of Night 148
Craft, Christopher 29, 88, 122
Cunningham, Michael,
The Hours 148

Dalziel, Pamela 144
dandyism 28–32
Darwin, Charles 75–6
On the Origin of Species 22, 23, 31, 72, 76, 123–6
Darwin, Erasmus 23
David, Deirdre 43, 47
Davidoff, Leonore 108
Davis, Lance 35
Davis, Philip 22
Dennis, Barbara 20
Dickens, Charles 12, 13, 17, 37–8, 53, 57, 101, 114, 123, 124, 132, 136, 137, 142, 143, 147, 148, 152, 153, 154
Bleak House 54, 64
A Christmas Carol 124
David Copperfield 79, 100
Dombey and Son 79, 100
Great Expectations 42, 100, 142
Hard Times 41, 55
Household Words 4, 55
Little Dorrit 18, 128
The Mystery of Edwin Drood 122, 142
Nicholas Nickleby 100
The Old Curiosity Shop 16
Oliver Twist 3, 11, 12, 16, 25, 31, 40, 41, 43, 47, 51–3, 57, 60, 64–6, 70, 75, 78, 79–81, 85, 97, 100, 103–4, 105, 113, 117, 129–30, 134, 138, 150
Our Mutual Friend 13–14, 43, 105, 122
The Pickwick Papers 38
A Tale of Two Cities 42
Dickens World (Kent, UK) 138
Dickinson, Emily 118
Disraeli, Benjamin 12, 35–6, 120
Dolling-Mann, Patricia,
Weatherbury Farm 144
Douglas, Lord Alfred 29
Dowling, Linda 28
Doyle, Arthur Conan (Sir) 39, 64, 100
Drew, John 153
Du Maurier, George,
Trilby 120

Eagleton, Terry 5, 41, 113–16
Eastlake, Elizabeth (Lady) 127
ecocriticism 128–31
Eldridge Pope (brewers) 143

Elementary Education Act (1870) 19, 46, 135
Eliot, George 12, 28, 40, 41, 43, 101, 114, 118, 120, 132, 143
Adam Bede 40, 122
Daniel Deronda 125
Middlemarch 67, 125
The Mill on the Floss 3, 24, 27, 60–2, 67–9, 72–5, 77, 84, 93–4, 103, 123–6, 133, 134
Silas Marner 128
'Silly Novels by Lady Novelists' 67, 107
Eliot, Simon 37, 38
Elizabeth I 35
Engels, Friedrich 63
The Englishwoman's Yearbook 54
Erwin, Sherri Browning, *Jane Slayre* 150

Faber, Michel, *The Crimson Petal and the White* 147
Factory Act (1833) 19
Factory Act (1850) 55
Factory Act (1856) 55
Festival of Britain (1951) 137
Filippo, Paul di, *Victoria* 150
Flanagan, Richard, *Wanting* 142
Flint, Kate 9, 67
Flynn, Suzanne J. 46
Forster's Education Act *see* Elementary Education Act
Foucault, Michel 5, 109, 121–3
Fowles, John, *The French Lieutenant's Woman* 140, 146–7
Fraiman, Susan 116
Franklin, Jane (Lady) 142
Franklin, John (Sir) 142
Fraser, George MacDonald, *Flashman* 140
Fraser's Magazine 27
Freedgood, Elaine 104
Furneaux, Holly 122

Gagnier, Regenia 128
Gallagher, Catherine 105
Gardiner, John 146
Garrad, Greg 129, 134
Gaskell, Elizabeth 41, 128, 148
Mary Barton 16, 43, 79, 124, 129, 133, 154
North and South 3, 17, 21, 23, 24, 40, 43, 47–8, 53–7, 62–4, 69, 77, 82–3, 85–7, 93–5, 100, 106–7, 115, 143
Ruth 79
Gelev, Penko 150
Gilbert, Pamela K. 47
Gilbert, Sandra M. 106, 118–19, 140
Gilman, Sander L. 120
Gilmour, Robin 20, 47, 94, 140–2
Girard, René 90
Girton Girl 71
Gissing, George 38, 45, 135
The Nether World 32
New Grub Street 136
The Odd Women 26
Goethe, Johann Wolfgang von 39
Gosse, Edmund 135, 143
Grahame-Smith, Seth, *Pride and Prejudice and Zombies* 150
Grand, Sarah 26
Grass, Sean 123
Great Exhibition (1851) 35, 137, 143
Great Reform Act (1832) 10, 14
Greg, W. R., 'Why are Women Redundant?' 27

Gubar, Susan 106, 118–19, 140
Guy, Josephine 105

Hager, Kelly 78
Haggard, Henry Rider 36, 39, 100
King Solomon's Mines 136
She 136
Halberstam, Judith 96
Hall, Catherine 108
Hallam, Arthur Henry 73
Hardy, Thomas 12, 38, 41, 114, 124, 136, 143, 144
Far From the Madding Crowd 4
'Geographical Knowledge' 131
Jude the Obscure 22, 90, 131
The Mayor of Casterbridge 4, 16, 23, 45, 60–2, 69, 75–6, 84–5, 90–3, 99–100, 104, 107, 113, 125, 130, 133, 134
Tess of the d'Urbervilles 62, 84, 104, 125
Harkness, Margaret,
In Darkest London 32
Hartley, Jenny 79
Heilmann, Ann 151
Henty, G. A. 36
Herbert, Christopher 34, 120–1, 133
Himmelfarb, Gertrude 13
Holman, Roger 139
homosexuality 28–32
Hopkins, Gerard Manley 124
Huang, Yu-ting 149
Hudson, George 18
Huttenback, Robert 35

Indian 'Mutiny' (1857, First Indian War of Independence) 35–7
Irish Famine 21
Irons, Jeremy 146
Irving, Henry 30

Jack the Ripper 32–4, 120, 138, 141
James, Henry 44, 136
Jenkins, Alice 151
John, Juliet 151
Jones, Lloyd,
Mister Pip 142
Joyce, Simon 151

Keble, John 21
Kettle, Arnold 116
Kincaid, James 122
Kingsley, Charles 148
The Water-Babies 124
Kipling, Rudyard 36
Kirchkopf, Andrea 147
Knight, Mark 48, 105
Kohlke, Marie-Luise 154
Kove, Seth 33
Kramer, Dale 91
Kreilkamp, Ivan 129

La Marck, Jean-Baptiste de 23
Labouchère Amendment (1885) 29–30
Landow, George 155
Lane, Lauriat 120
Laver, James 137–8
Le Fanu, Sheridan,
Carmilla 145
Lean, David,
Oliver Twist (dir.) 14
Leary, Patrick 152, 154
Ledger, Sally 46, 72, 87, 88, 116
Levine, George 2, 37, 42, 126
Lewes, Agnes 103
Lewes, George Henry 103, 125
Lewis, Sarah 127
Linton, Eliza Lynn 87
Litvack, Leon 153
Llewellyn, Mark 141, 150–1
Lodge, David,
Nice Work 143, 148–9

Lombroso, Cesare 31, 76
London Society for the Protection of Young Females and the Prevention of Prostitution 80
Lonoff, Sue 132
Lyell, Charles,
Principles of Geology 22

Malam, John 150
Malthus, Thomas 124
Manchester Mechanics' Institute 38
Manchester Working Men's College 38
Mangum, Teresa 129
Marcus, Steven 122
Marshall, Gail 26
Martineau, Harriet 35
Marx, Karl 125
Mason, Emma 48, 105
Matsuoka, Mitsuharu 154
May, Simon 139
Mayhew, Henry,
London Labour and the London Poor 78–9
McCarthy, Patrick 153
McCrea, Barry 122
Miller, D. A. 123
Miller, J. Hillis 147
Mitchell, Sally 47
Moore, George 38
Moore, Grace 129–30, 137, 148
Moretti, Franco 39–40, 95–6
Morgentaler, Goldie 120
Morris, Pam 42, 47
Morris, William 139
Morrison, Arthur,
The Child of the Jago 32
Morse, Deborah Denenholz 100
Mudie, Charles 37
Mudie's Circulating Library 37
Mukherjee, Upamanyu Pablo 132
Myers, Janet C. 97

Naidu, Sarojini 132
National Review 27
National Society for Women's Suffrage 26
naturalism 45
Neo-Victorianism 5, 9, 139–52
Newman, John Henry 21, 22
The Idea of a University 94
Newnes, George 39
Newport Rising 15
Nightingale, Florence 126
Nord, Deborah Epstein 86
Nordau, Max 31, 76
Norton, Caroline (Lady) 126
Nosferatu 146

O'Gorman, Francis 105
Oxford Movement 21

Pall Mall Gazette 29, 122
Palliser, Charles,
The Quincunx 147–8
Parker, Pamela Corpron 54
Parr, Andrew 146
Parson, Deborah 85
Peters, Laura 51
Pierce-Jones, Roy 144
Pite, Ralph 5, 130–1
Plotz, John 17, 117
Polanski, Roman,
Tess 144
Politi, Jina 116
Poor Law Amendment Act (1834) 13, 51, 114
Poovey, Mary 5, 105, 126–8, 133
Potter, Dennis 144
Pulham, Patricia 150–1
Punch 33
Pusey, Edmund 21

Queer theory 122

Ragussis, Michael 120

Reform Act (1832) 10, 14
Reform Act (1867) 10
Renk, Kathleen J. 150
Representation of the People Act (1884) 10
Rhodes, Cecil 35
Rhys, Jean,
Wide Sargasso Sea 118–19, 139–40
Rice, Anne 145
Richard, Cliff,
Heathcliff 139
Richards, Thomas 132
Richardson, Angelique 72, 125
Ritvo, Harriet 129
Rossetti, Christina 149, 154
Rowlatt, Chris 150
Ruskin, John 124
'Of Queen's Gardens' 19–20

Sackville-West, Vita 136
Said, Edward W. 34, 57, 116, 118
Salvation Army 31
Schaffer, Talia 27, 29, 89
Schlesinger, John,
Far from the Madding Crowd 144
Scott, Walter (Sir) 139
Sedgwick, Eve Kosofsky 29, 122
Seeley, John (Sir) 34
Seltzer, Mark 33
separate spheres 24
Sesame Street 146
Sharpe, Jenny 119–20
Shattock, Joanne 131–2
Shaw, George Bernard 135
Showalter, Elaine 30, 31, 91, 93, 118
Shuttleworth, Sally 107, 126
Simmons, Dan,
Drood 142
Sinfield, Alan 122
Smiles, Samuel,
Self Help 39, 94
Smith, Shelia M. 13, 105
Smith, William Robertson,
The Religion of the Semites 121
Spencer, Herbert 123
Spivak, Gayatri Chakravorty 5, 117–19
Stead, W. T.,
The Maiden Tribute of Modern Babylon 29, 122
steampunk 150
Stendhal, (Marie-Henri Behle),
The Red and the Black 39
Stephen, Leslie (Sir) 137
Stevenson, Robert Louis,
The Strange Case of Dr. Jekyll and Mr. Hyde 30
Stoker, Bram,
Dracula 4, 11, 27, 29–30, 34, 44–5, 48, 66, 71–2, 76–7, 87–90, 92, 95–7, 100, 108, 120, 121, 129, 133, 136, 145
Stoneman, Patsy 142–3
Strachey, Lytton 136
Strand, The (magazine) 39

Taylor, Miles 131
Taylor, Philip Meadows,
Confessions of a Thug 35
Tennant, Emma,
Tess 144
Tennyson, Alfred, Lord,
The Idylls of the King 30
In Memoriam 23, 73
Tests and Corporations Act (1828) 21
Thacker, David 144
Thackeray, William, Makepeace 35
Vanity Fair 127, 136
Thomas, Ronald 146
Thomas, Sue 120
Tosh, John 90, 95
Tractarian Movement 21
Tranchall, Peter 144

Trollope, Anthony 120, 137
The Way We Live Now 18
Twilight 146

utilitarianism 13

Victoria, Queen 1, 9, 25, 35–6, 37, 135
Diamond Jubilee (1897) 36
Golden Jubilee (1887) 36

Walkowitz, Judith 122
Waller, John 14
'Walter',
My Secret Life 121
Waters, Catherine 108
Waters, Sarah,
Tipping the Velvet 147
Watt, Ian 77
Webber, Andrew Lloyd (Lord),
I'd Do Anything (BBC) 139
The Woman in White 138
Weedon, Alexis 38, 47
Weiss, Barbara 17
Wells, H. G. 45
The Time Machine 44
The War of the Worlds 44
Westminster Review 123
WH Smith (book seller) 38
Wheeler, Michael 47
Whitby Abbey (Yorkshire, UK) 138
Whitechapel Murders 32–4
Whitman, Walt 29–30
Wilde, Oscar 29, 136
The Importance of Being Earnest 135
Lady Windermere's Fan 135
Wildhorn, Frank,
Dracula, the Musical 146
Williams, Raymond 11, 60, 116, 118, 130
Wills, W. H. 4
Winterbottom, Michael,
The Claim 144–5
Wisnicki, Adrian 132
Wohl, Anthony S. 108
Wolff, Larry 80, 122
Wollstonecraft, Mary,
Vindication of the Rights of Woman 26
Woolf, Virginia,
'Mr. Bennett and Mrs. Brown' 136
Orlando 1, 24, 136–7
Wordsworth, William,
The Prelude 11

Year of Revolutions (1848) 17

Zanger, Jules 34, 120, 133
Zieger, Susan 122
Ziemba, Paul 146
Zola, Emile 45